We are the first people who are leaving nothing for our children – and America is leading the charge. We are at war against our children.

Ariane Mnouchkine
New York, July 22, 2005

Frontispiece Ariane Mnouchkine and the Théâtre du Soleil at the Cartoucherie de Vincennes during the run of *The Shakespeare Cycle*, 1981

ARIANE MNOUCHKINE

Routledge Performance Practitioners is a series of introductory guides to the key theater-makers of the last century. Each volume explains the background to and the work of one of the major influences on twentieth- and twenty-first-century performance.

Ariane Mnouchkine, the most significant living French theater director, has devised over the last forty years a form of research and creation with her theater collective, Le Théâtre du Soleil, that is both engaged with contemporary history and committed to reinvigorating theater by foregrounding the centrality of the actor. This is the first book to combine:

- an overview of Mnouchkine's life, work and theatrical influences
- an exploration of her key ideas on theater and the creative process
- analysis of key productions, including her early and groundbreaking environmental political piece, *1789*, and the later Asian-inspired play penned by Hélène Cixous, *Drums on the Dam*
- practical exercises, including tips on mask work.

As a first step toward critical understanding, and as an initial exploration before going on to further, primary research, **Routledge Performance Practitioners** are unbeatable value for today's student.

Judith G. Miller is Chair and Professor of French and Francophone Theatre in the Department of French at New York University.

ROUTLEDGE PERFORMANCE PRACTITIONERS

Series editor: Franc Chamberlain, University College Cork

Routledge Performance Practitioners is an innovative series of introductory handbooks on key figures in twentieth-century performance practice. Each volume focuses on a theater-maker whose practical and theoretical work has in some way transformed the way we understand theater and performance. The books are carefully structured to enable the reader to gain a good grasp of the fundamental elements underpinning each practitioner's work. They will provide an inspiring springboard for future study, unpacking and explaining what can initially seem daunting.

The main sections of each book cover:

- personal biography
- explanation of key writings
- description of significant productions
- reproduction of practical exercises.

Volumes currently available in the series are:

Konstantin Stanislavsky by Bella Merlin
Hijikata Tatsumi and Ohno Kazuo by Sondra Fraleigh and
    Tamah Nakamura
Robert Wilson by Maria Shevtsova

Future volumes will include:

Antonin Artaud
Pina Bausch
Bertolt Brecht
Peter Brook
Rudolf Laban
Robert Lepage
Lee Strasberg
Mary Wigman

ARIANE
MNOUCHKINE

Judith G. Miller

Routledge
Taylor & Francis Group

LONDON AND NEW YORK

First published 2007
by Routledge
2 Park Square, Milton Park, Abingdon, Oxon OX14 4RN

Simultaneously published in the USA and Canada
by Routledge
270 Madison Ave, New York, NY 10016

*Routledge is an imprint of the Taylor & Francis Group,
an informa business*

Typeset in Perpetua by
Newgen Imaging Systems (P) Ltd, Chennai, India
Printed and bound in Great Britain by
Antony Rowe Ltd, Chippenham, Wiltshire

British Library Cataloguing in Publication Data
A catalogue record for this book is available from
the British Library

Library of Congress Cataloging in Publication Data
Miller, Judith Graves.
    Ariane Mnouchkine / by Judith G. Miller
        p. cm.—(Routledge performance practitioners)
    Includes bibliographical references and index.
        1. Mnouchkine, Ariane, 1938—Critism and interpretation.
    I. Title.
    PN2638.M445M55 2007
    792.023'3092—dc22   2006034409

ISBN10: 0–415–33884–0 (hbk)
ISBN10: 0–415–33885–9 (pbk)
ISBN10: 0–203–44847–2 (ebk)

ISBN13: 978–0–415–33884–4 (hbk)
ISBN13: 978–0–415–33885–1 (pbk)
ISBN13: 978–0–203–44847–2 (ebk)

TO THE MEMORY OF GREAT TEACHERS AND FRIENDS WHO HAVE INSPIRED ME BY THEIR OWN PASSIONS TO PURSUE WHAT I LOVE: DENIS BABLET, TIM COOK, CLAIRE DUCHEN, ELIZABETH KARLAN, ILSE LIPSCHUTZ, MARY LYDON, ELAINE MARKS, AND YVONNE OZZELLO

CONTENTS

FIGURES

ACKNOWLEDGMENTS

Ariane Mnouchkine's theater work has accompanied and inspired me ever since I first set foot in France in 1967. I have seen all but two of her post-1967 productions, and many of them several times. I undertook this study of Mnouchkine, then, despite my seemingly all-embracing move to New York City and a new job, because I could not imagine not being in her company. For sparking the thinking and creativity that went into this book, I therefore thank first the intrepid director she is. I also thank all the Théâtre du Soleil family, past and present, for teaching me about what theater can do and be. From this community, I especially thank Hélène Cixous who, with her knowingness, brings me ever closer to understanding Ariane Mnouchkine's gifts. I thank, too, Jean-François Dusigne and Lucia Bensasson, Directors of ARTA at the Cartoucherie de Vincennes, who shared some of their acting experience as former members of the Théâtre du Soleil during a long interview in the summer of 2003.

Without discussing and producing theater in French, including the Soleil's *1789*, with my students – first at The University of Wisconsin-Madison, then at New York University in France and now at the main campus of New York University, my insights and my energy for living would not be the same. I am grateful to them, too, as well as to my stimulating colleagues and staff in both New York University settings. I am also deeply moved that so many former students are involved in the world of teaching and theater-making.

For many years of probing conversations about theater work, about France, about meaningful political choices, and notably about Ariane Mnouchkine, I would like to acknowledge here my longtime friends and colleagues: David Bradby, Michal Govrin, Allen Kuharski, Kate Turley, Philippa Wehle, and Jack Yeager. For their superb contributions to Mnouchkine studies, I thank Josette Féral, Béatrice Picon-Vallin, and David Williams.

The Magnum Agency has allowed me to include in this book the photography of Martine Franck, who, since the company's inception, has documented brilliantly the productions of the Théâtre du Soleil. All photos are thus courtesy of Martine Franck/Magnum Photos. Spending long hours at Magnum-Paris in preparation for this book, pouring over at least a thousand production shots of the Théâtre du Soleil, made me feel as though I was reviewing my own life in French theater. I thank the Magnum staff for their hospitality in indulging my nostalgia, and also for helping to jog my critical memory.

For the completion of this manuscript, I owe the greatest debt to Helen Richardson, who wrote the original version of Chapter 4: Practical Exercises, and thus anchored the existing chapter, its content based largely on her sensitivity and experience. Helen's own work on Mnouchkine, her many years as an international theater director, her painstaking and joyful theatrical collaboration with her own students, always in the spirit of Mnouchkine, made it possible to suggest approaches to theater-making that resonate with the work of the Théâtre du Soleil.

Franc Chamberlain, editor for this Routledge series, Talia Rodgers, publisher of Routledge's Theatre and Performance Studies, and Minh Ha Duong, development editor, gently encouraged, abetted, and supported the project from the outset. I thank them for this and for their patience.

I would like to conclude these prefatory remarks with a word about translations and other editorial matters. Unless otherwise noted, all of the translations from the French (from play texts, interviews, and articles) are my own. I have left in French the titles of Mnouchkine's and the Théâtre du Soleil's productions that have never been published in English translation, notably Hélène Cixous' 1987 play, *l'Indiade ou l'Inde de leurs rêves*, which could be rendered as "The Indiad or India of Their Dreams." Other such titles and possible translations include those of the plays *Les Clowns* [The Clowns], 1969; *1793 ou la cité révolutionnaire est de ce monde* [1793 or The Revolutionary City is of Our Times], 1973; *l'Age d'Or: première ébauche* [The Age of Gold: First Draft], 1975; *Et Soudain des nuits d'éveil*

[And Suddenly Wakeful Nights], 1997; and *Le Dernier Caravansérail* [The Last Caravanserai], 2003. I signal, in addition, titles of the made-for-television film *La Nuit miraculeuse* [The Miraculous Night], 1989 and the film of Mnouchkine's rehearsals of *Tartuffe*, *Au Soleil même la nuit* [With The Soleil Even at Night], 1997. It might be useful to note that *Drums on the Dam*, which is the published translation of the title of Hélène Cixous' play, *Tambours sur la digue*, was given as "The Flood Drummers" while the production toured in Australia and New Zealand. I have included at the end of the volume a glossary of terms and proper names, bolded in the text, to help contextualize important references with which readers may not be familiar. I hope that other such historical or theatrical references will be easily grasped from chapter content or from readers' overall cultural backgrounds.

INTELLECTUAL AND ARTISTIC BIOGRAPHY

Nomad of the imagination

Ariane Mnouchkine cultivates obvious paradoxes. Too many women are mixed up in her: the leader of a theatre company who founds with her student pals from the Sorbonne in 1964 the workers' cooperative of the Théâtre du Soleil and the writer-poet of sweet and luminous phrases; the flamboyant filmmaker of *Molière* and the meticulous caretaker of the Cartoucherie who can't delegate anything; the visionary director and the actors' nurse-confessor; the educator and the *gourmande*; the general and the little girl; the militant and the hedonist; the saint and the adventuress. [...] a character out of the ordinary for a company out of the normal! An out-of-the-ordinary story.

(Pascaud 2005: 211–12)

Fabienne Pascaud's robust description of French director Ariane Mnouchkine sums up not only the paradoxes Mnouchkine herself cultivates but also hints at the contradictions through which she has lived. For the last half of the twentieth century and beginning of the twenty-first have seen both the heights of entrepreneurial artistic possibilities combined with utopian social dreams, *and* the dizzying multiplication of military aggression, internecine warfare, political exile, and genocide. In the especially sensitive way of most artists, Mnouchkine has resonated with all these historical moments, demonstrating, moreover, in her work with the Théâtre du Soleil a dedication to engaging with history that has never wavered. She has also evinced an extreme vulnerability and the potential for rough and tumble leadership, a selfless commitment to political militancy, and a desire for complete immersion in the creative realm. What has been constant is her unassailable practice of theater as an act of faith in humanity, gifting audience and actors with something "so incredibly rare" (Féral 1998: 159) that she has become France's most celebrated contemporary director. Given the exceptionally male-dominated milieu of French theater, the story of her success is all the more compelling.

A part of the generation that was born into the Second World War, Mnouchkine began her life with the defeat of France by German forces and in the moral quagmire which ensued when Germany occupied the country. She came into adulthood, however, in the midst of "*Les trente glorieuses*," or the greatest stretch of prosperity and growth in French history. This halcyon period also came with attendant anxieties, notably the complications of transforming a mostly rural France into a suburban nation. She saw the decline of France as a world power with the end of French colonization and the ugliness of two colonial wars in the 1950s (Indochina and Algeria). But she also saw France become a key player in the European Union, striving toward European independence from American economic and cultural hegemony.

To come to grips with Mnouchkine's interconnected creative genius and political activism, it is crucial to examine her life, the life of her split centuries, and the theatrical currents within which she has situated and distinguished herself, becoming with the Théâtre du Soleil what critic Denis Bablet already saw in 1979, "the most important adventure in French theatre since Jean Vilar and his **Théâtre National Populaire**" (Bablet 1979: 88). In the following, sections, we will endeavor to capture the way in which familial, political, and intellectual contexts have acted upon Mnouchkine, the artist, while sketching how she has also acted both upon and with her times.

BEGINNINGS

HER FATHER'S DAUGHTER

Ariane Mnouchkine came into the world and into a cosmopolitan and artistic household on March 3, 1939. Her father, Alexandre Mnouchkine, who was born in Russia and exiled with his family to Paris in 1925 as a consequence of the Russian Revolution, was to become one of France's most important post-war film producers. Her mother, the actor Jane Hannen, hailed from a British family of diplomats and performers, her own father having acted at the Old Vic with Lawrence Olivier. Although Mnouchkine speaks rarely of her mother, she credits her with great storytelling skills, fueling the young Ariane's imagination by her ability to conjure up a perfectly credible fantasy world of Celtic spirits. Her father, on the other hand, clearly holds pride of place in her personal development: "At every moment of my life the only thing of which I was entirely certain was that my father loved me" (Pascaud 2005: 26–7).

The mainstay of her life until his death in 1993, Alexandre Mnouchkine, with his production partner Georges Dancigers, helped finance the beginning efforts of the Théâtre du Soleil, produced the filmed version of the Soleil's first international theatrical triumph, *1789* (1974), and contributed the last necessary funding for the expressionistic *Molière* (1976) – Ariane Mnouchkine's only feature-length fiction film and one that can be read as a meditation on the glory of a theater company's itinerant life and the inevitable intensity of a creative community. Alexandre Mnouchkine did far more, however, than support her efforts financially. He placed her at the heart of his own work by naming his company, "Les films Ariane," gave her a role in several of his ventures, including asking her to collaborate on the screenplay for *The Man from Rio* (1964), and became her best friend and most cantankerous sparring partner.

From her first contact as an adolescent with her father's colorfully melodramatic and adventure-filled film work, a case in point being the swashbuckling *Fanfan la Tulipe* with Gérard Philippe (1952), it would seem that Mnouchkine developed an affinity for larger than life gestures and sumptuous and physically arresting images. She, herself, tells the family story that has haunted her since childhood and imprinted her aesthetic with her father's experience. In 1919 and 1920, her father and his sister Galina spent two years endlessly zigzagging across Russia's great north in an attempt to escape the ravages of the Russian Revolution. One night, from the window of the train in which they were riding, the two children saw an entire army frozen to death but still moving. Wrapped in the splendid golden vestments they had pillaged from a monastery, the dead soldiers advanced on small horses that would not stop trotting. Mnouchkine comments, "I think that that vision inscribed itself in [my father] and then in me forever. Revolution. War. Apocalypse.

The mystery of those Asian faces" (Pascaud 2005: 45). In her assessment of the importance of this story, already filtered through her father's imagination, we see how Mnouchkine thinks in images, how the visual world captures the emotions and concepts she holds dearest and most wishes to communicate.

Mnouchkine also inherited from her father the courage to innovate and switch gears, as he did when he moved from producing surrealist fantasies (Cocteau's *The Eagle Has Two Heads* 1948) to crowd-pleasers (*Cartouche* 1962) to the New Wave-affiliated films of Claude Lelouche, *Live for Life*, 1967. Like her father, Mnouchkine has been able to push the limits of what she knows about her art, in her case, recalibrating space, form, and time, without agonizing over whether or not the work will "sell." Like him, Mnouchkine discovered from her work with film technicians how much she loved laboring over details, becoming expert in all aspects of production, and working tirelessly wherever needed. Alexandre Mnouchkine's world of writers, poets, arts' entrepreneurs, creative and gutsy performers, and thinkers became hers forever. Indeed, the film director Claude Lelouche, whose films Alexandre Mnouchkine also distributed, joined Ariane Mnouchkine as partner in forming in 1979 the pressure group AIDA (l'Association Internationale des Droits d'Artistes) to call attention to dissident and radical artists silenced or jailed by repressive political regimes.

Although her parents divorced when she was thirteen, Mnouchkine recalls a spirited and united young family defying the powers of destruction all around them. Hiding out in the early 1940s in Bordeaux from the German occupying forces, father, mother, and children watched from their yard the spectacle of falling bombs, rather than cowering in their basement. Destruction, nevertheless, engulfed her Jewish grandparents still living in Paris. Denounced by their concierge, they were deported and gassed, their story emblematic of some 83,000 Jews living in France at the time, victims of the Holocaust. Their fate haunts many of Mnouchkine's later productions, either overtly – as in her only authored play, *Méphisto* (1979), adapted from Klaus Mann's novel castigating the rise of Nazism in Hamburg in the 1930s – or covertly – as in the melancholic and eerie cemetery setting of Hélène Cixous' AIDS-play *The Perjured City* (1994), or in the focus on other genocidal situations in productions such as *The Terrible But Unfinished Story of Norodom Sihanouk, King of Cambodia* (Cixous 1985), *l'Indiade* (Cixous 1987), and *Le Dernier Caravansérail* (2003). Of her own Jewishness, Mnouchkine allows that she was never educated in a Jewish tradition, a lack of structure she found liberating. Yet, she also identifies with being Jewish: "I didn't and still don't have any Jewish culture. But the only problem is I feel Jewish every time a Jew does something terrible or when someone does something terrible to a Jew. That means almost all of the time" (Pascaud 2005: 38). Her frustration is yet another indication of her deep empathy for victims of discrimination, political violence, and marginalization, a sensitivity that manifests itself both in the subjects of her plays and in her activism. More concretely, she finds herself evoking her Jewishness since the late 1990s, along with her support of Palestinian rights, as a response to the meanness contaminating the social field in France over the Israeli–Palestinian situation.

THEATER AS A CALLING

As much as being involved in the cinema work of her father helped educate and form her tastes, the compromises necessary to realizing a film repulsed her. She had, however, long thrilled to the richness of the international theater productions she had experienced as a girl in the late 1950s at Paris' **Théâtre des Nations**. She indeed went there to see **Giorgio Strehler**'s version of Pirandello's *Giants of the Mountain* eleven times, as well as to have her first taste of **kathakali** theater. Strehler's precision choreography and luscious color sense and the physical mastery of the kathakali performers she had seen had already begun to have an impact on her own aesthetic when the choice of theater as a vocation hit her as a veritable *coup de foudre* during a study-abroad year at Oxford University. Working on several productions in 1957, under the direction of fellow students Ken Loach and John McGrath (later, a fervent partisan of the Théâtre du Soleil), convinced her that a life in the theater could provide the focus for her burgeoning desire to define creativity as a collective effort and to use this creativity to affect some kind of change in the world.

To these ends and while still a student of psychology at the Sorbonne, she founded ATEP (l'Association Théâtrale des Etudiants Parisiens) in 1959, under the patronage of **Roger Planchon**. A rival theater group to the much longer established student association for classical theater (Le Théâtre Antique de la Sorbonne), Mnouchkine's group, which would later form the core of Le Théâtre du Soleil, sought to explore the contemporary rapport between theater and society. In the thick of the **Algerian War**, ATEP sponsored incendiary lectures by **Jean-Paul Sartre** and on **Jean Genet**'s dramas. It produced, in 1961 in the Arènes de Lutèce, *Genghis Khan* written by Mnouchkine's early mentor Henri Bauchau. This was Mnouchkine's first and untutored attempt at a grand scale historical epic with outsized historical figures.

Of this period, the most significant and unquestionably life-changing experience was Mnouchkine's decision at age twenty-three to take a year off and explore Asia. What she saw in 1962–3 would orient, especially after 1980, her approach to theatrical form. Hélène Cixous, company author and principle collaborator, thinks that Mnouchkine's trip "was an initiatory voyage, [which] stayed with her as a book of images" (Prenowitz 2004: 19). The trip, the first of many in years to come – improvised, serendipitous, sometimes frightening, always stimulating – brought her in contact with what she has come to believe are the roots of true theater: powerful iconic visual imagery, physical acumen based on intensive training and imitation of master players, joyous and direct contact with an audience for whom the experience of theater is as necessary to life as water. Traveling alone most of the time, she took some astonishing photos of people and performers in Japan, India, Pakistan, Cambodia, Taiwan, Afghanistan, Turkey, and Iran. She would meet up occasionally with her friend Martine Franck, who was to become a lifelong artistic partner and the official photographer of Le Théâtre du Soleil. Perhaps their aesthetic complementarity – Mnouchkine's opulent costuming and vibrant colors and Franck's chiaroscuro lighting effects and dramatic framing – derives from that time.

THE RISING OF THE THÉÂTRE DU SOLEIL

Like many other European theater companies emerging in the 1960s, the Théâtre du Soleil was created in reaction to what was felt to be a hyper-commercialization of theater and thus a loss of theater's ability to move and instruct audiences. Many youthful artists believed that theater had become, on the whole, just another object of consumption: "Theatre can't make up its mind what it is. It's boring. It has nothing more to say. It's lost the audience" (Carré 1985: 147). However, unlike most of its sister companies in France, the Soleil set out not only to shake up the themes but also to revolutionize the institutional and creative aspects of French theater. The members were indeed laughed at when explaining what they wanted to do, even charged by the actors' union with amateurism. Nevertheless, in 1964 they forged ahead with plans to establish a workers' cooperative and to create texts adhering to the actors' real-life engagement with society and politics.

Formed as a cooperative by the original nine members, with each member contributing 900 francs, the Soleil practiced (and still practices) the same salary for each member – in 2005, 1,677 euros a month – regardless of the kind of work done. In the first phase of their creative research during the summer of 1964, they traveled to the rural Ardèche region of France to raise sheep and do theater, experimenting with a Stanislavskian approach to characterization. They returned to Paris for their first production, Gorki's *The Petty Bourgeoisie* (1964–5), a kind of exorcism of what they might have become had they hewed to the expectations of their social class. Moving toward championing a collective approach to creating texts, they turned to Gautier's *Captain Fracasse* in 1966, with Mnouchkine and company member Philippe Léotard writing scenes based on improvisations culled from specific moments in the novel. Life was still stressful. Despite the success of the boldly performed, cabaret-like *Fracasse*, actors and technicians had to have day jobs to survive. They could only rehearse at night.

Nevertheless, given the French government's exceptional interest in theater in the 1960s, it was relatively easy in terms of bureaucracy for the Soleil to get launched. The climate created by Culture Minister André Malraux, who encouraged the arts as crucial to national prestige, meant that there was a cadre of professional experts ready to see all new young companies' work and promote it. If deemed worthy, as was the Soleil, a young company was modestly subsidized. The Soleil thus received enough money from the government in 1967 to pay for sets and costumes, and eventually in 1970 a leg up when the time came to find a permanent home. Mnouchkine and the Soleil also benefited in their first years from generous godfathers, most of whom would later appear in cameo roles in her film *Molière*. Seasoned theater men who believed in the company and helped with moral support, theater space, and advice (Jean Vilar, **Jean-Louis Barrault**, Paolo Grassi of Milan's Piccolo Theater, Roger Planchon, and theater critic Alfred Simon, among others) remained unwavering in their enthusiasm for the new vision of theater the company represented.

Evolution within the Théâtre du Soleil

From this early period, Mnouchkine's role within the company has evolved. She has held the Soleil together, weathered the departure of all the other original members, and emerged as the teacher, inspirer, and "mother." From 1980 on, she has regularly sponsored free workshops to keep her own actors growing and also to discover new talent for the next production. She has also spearheaded the transformation of the Soleil's theater and the complex which houses it, the Cartoucherie de Vincennes, from an abandoned armaments factory into the principle site for experimental theater in France. Hers has been a reclamation project that has given back to Paris, through an enormous investment of manual labor and artistic meaning, a wondrous space on the city's eastern fringes that had been scheduled in the early 1970s to be destroyed. In 1970, when the Soleil, with the complicity of Paris' municipal counsel, squatted their three-hangared locale, the members were alone with their problems of plumbing, heating, infrastructure, and transportation. Today the Cartoucherie comprises five fully functioning and cooperating theaters in a vast, welcoming, and bucolic park, and a theater training school, ARTA, L'Association de Recherche de Traditions de l'Acteur, that Mnouchkine founded in 1989 to offer workshops in non-Western theater techniques.

MNOUCHKINE AND HER TIMES

MNOUCHKINE, THE SOLEIL, AND SOCIOPOLITICS

To recount the history of the Théâtre du Soleil is to take note of many of the major political upsets and events of the 1960s to the present. The company has evolved in symbiosis with, and in reaction to, the so-called Revolution of May 68; the coming to power of the Socialists with the government of François Mitterand (1981–95); the fall of the Berlin Wall and the decline of communism (late 1980s); and the end of colonialism and the rise of postcolonial geopolitical turmoil (l970s to the present). The latter includes the formation of a new Europe and a forced and often illegal immigration that is shifting the cultural boundaries of peoples and nations. Of these enumerated events, it was undoubtedly the upheaval of May 68 that crystallized the early mission of the company.

MAY 68 AND THE THÉÂTRE DU SOLEIL

Just four years old, the Théâtre du Soleil was performing *A Midsummer Night's Dream* when a combined student and worker social-action movement shut down universities, factories, state transportation and communication systems, and theaters – and nearly toppled the conservative government of the Second World War hero, General Charles De Gaulle. France, already in difficulty over its inadequate educational system, and in the throes of an identity crisis over its role in a world dominated by an economically voracious United States, erupted in a series of strikes, rallies, and demonstrations. Students, in particular, were incensed over the atrocities of the war in Vietnam. Protests ranged from serious and volatile discussions between different Marxist factions in designated open forums to anarchist performances and acts of "liberation" (from wildcat postering to torching cars) in the streets.

Like other Left-leaning theater groups (most of France's theater world at the time, in fact), the Soleil participated in the events of May through what was termed an "active strike." Closing down its performances of Shakespeare, it chose to restage in striking factories Arnold Wesker's *The Kitchen* – its 1967 production that had proven to be a watershed experience in developing physical discipline, in part thanks to lessons learned from Mnouchkine via her classes with Jacques Lecoq. The tightly choreographed movements of the kitchen workers had brought critics and spectators in droves to the Cirque Médrano, making *The Kitchen* one of the most remarked upon productions of the 1967 season and alleviating some of the company's financial worries.

In committing to the May 68 movement, the Soleil's goal was twofold: entertain the striking workers of Citroen, Kodak, and Renault – the factories where the company deployed its talents – and animate discussions about working conditions in highly stressful situations. The big commercial kitchen of the play provided an analogy with assembly-line work. Through performing, the Soleil helped the workers maintain their strike action in three weeks of direct contact. The company not only entertained but also listened to workers' concerns.

The Soleil's generally positive experience during May resulted in an awareness of the benefits of including members of the public in the process of creative work and an enthusiasm for delving into the political conundrums of the times. However, in the wake of the failure of May 68 to affect any concrete political change, the company, like many progressive arts groups, also felt it had to confront the impotency of the artist's role in society. Thus, in its immediate post-68 production, *Les Clowns* (1969), the Soleil – then some twenty-three members strong – self-consciously explored forms of individual creativity through improvised physical comedy. Mnouchkine led the way, selecting the final improvisations, and establishing the order of what became a satirical collage. The resulting production was polemical and only moderately successful.

On the other hand, the profoundly meaningful sojourn that had preceded the show in the summer of 1968 and that had taken place in the abandoned salt works built by Claude-Nicolas Ledoux at Arc-en-Senans had allowed the company to explore some of the ideals of the 68 revolt, notably communal existence and collective creation. By inviting local people to rehearsals, Mnouchkine had also experienced first hand the pleasure of improvising before a specific audience. Moreover, she retained from this experience the responsiveness of audience and actors to *commedia dell'arte* masks, and the possibility of letting go of detailed control to observe quietly and later comment on the actors' creativity. The lessons of Arc-en-Senans contributed to the realization of what are still among the most acclaimed and influential of the Soleil's productions, *1789* and *1793* (1970–3), the two-part collective rewriting of the French Revolution meant to help grasp the functioning of politics and economics through a deconstruction of the reigning myth of an egalitarian French nation. Responding to the debates unleashed during May 68, these two pieces denounce the rise of the bourgeoisie and the squelching of the popular classes after the French Revolution and explore the process by which a popular democracy might be able to take place.

Long-term effects of May 68 on Mnouchkine

May 68 can be understood as a point of coalescence for a number of important ideas alive in the French (and more generally Euro-American) intellectual firmament of the late 1950s through at least the late 1970s. We can posit certain of these as having a crucial impact on Mnouchkine's thinking and thus on the functioning of the Théâtre du Soleil. In the ubiquitous idea of process becoming more important than product, a notion that critic **Roland Barthes** would formulate as "writing replacing literature," we can see Mnouchkine's ability to spend months of rehearsal time improvising a production, putting off a start date, and even jeopardizing the financial health of the ensemble. This led her, for example, to produce a collective work in 1975 which she characterized as a "draft" (*L'Age d'Or:"première ébauche"*). Furthermore, to this day, Mnouchkine does not see her productions as "packages," but rather as encounters between two creative groups in a process of exchange.

Basic to Mnouchkine's approach to theater is the sense that theater work should not be alienating: It should insert the individual into a social whole, with everyone, and especially every artist, given the opportunity to speak out, to become a force for social change. This striving resonates with the hold that Brechtian theory had in the late 1950s and 1960s on the thinking of French theater people. The utopian thrust of a fully egalitarian society, including the new activist spectator theorized by **Louis Althusser**'s writings on Brecht's theater, permeated the way in which the Soleil structured itself and imagined its public. Nevertheless, Mnouchkine, all the while positioning herself on the Left, never proclaimed herself as part of a specific political movement nor has she ever cited **Bertolt Brecht** as a primary inspiration for her work.

> At the beginning we were "leftish," we knew we were, but we were not Brechtian nor communist. We were just looking for progress, freedom, and justice. We didn't have an ideology as such. But we were idealists. That means that we were not taken very seriously because we did not pretend to have a very strict Maoist, Trotskyte or Stalinist ideology. We were not leftists, just *"de gauche,"* and we still are. We never obeyed any dogma.
>
> (Delgado and Heritage 1996: 184)

While on the "Left," Mnouchkine has held fiercely onto her political autonomy and individualism. In this, we might also see the call for liberation from all dogma that underscored the events of 1968. The events of May 68 and the ambient progressive climate that continued to dominate the world of French arts in the 1970s and 1980s encouraged the Soleil, with Ariane Mnouchkine in the leadership role, to activate a desire for commitment to community, to work toward a form of coherency between artistic production and self-definition, and to conduct itself so as to insert its productions into the fabric of sociopolitical reality. Despite her musing about not being taken seriously as a young artist, Ariane Mnouchkine, in the French tradition of a Zola or a Sartre, emerged after May as a public intellectual, and thus a force with which to reckon. These days, everyone pays attention to her pronouncements on world politics as well as on art.

POLITICAL ACTIVISM

From the 1970s onwards, Mnouchkine and the Soleil have been on board with other activists for a range of social actions and street theater performances. For example, in 1973 the company created a sketch on behalf of the prison support group headed by **Michel Foucault** (Groupe d'Informations Prisons) seeking better conditions for prisoners. In 1981, the Soleil demonstrated for the Polish liberation movement, Solidarity. With AIDA, the international pressure group for artists' rights, Mnouchkine and the company have produced statements, sit-ins, and public spectacles in support, to name a few instances, of the then dissident Czech playwright Václev Haval (1981), Argentinian *desaparecidos* (1981), and Algerian artists caught up in civil war (1991). In 1971, Mnouchkine herself signed the now famous petition for legalized abortion sponsored by Simone de Beauvoir, among others, in which over 300 prominent French women declared they had undergone illegal abortions. In 1995, she went on a thirty-day hunger strike to protest France's non-intervention in the ethnic killings in Bosnia. In one of the Soleil's most sustained actions, the company offered refuge in 1996 to 382 mostly Malian illegal immigrants who had been expulsed from the St Bernard Church in Paris where they had sought asylum. The company's collective production, *Et soudain des nuits d'éveil* (1997), mirrors this experience by confronting the characters of theater-makers with the characters of illegal immigrants who invade the formers' theater, only to eventually return home. The Soleil's recent collective piece, *Le Dernier Caravansérail* (2003) resulted from Mnouchkine's personal investigations, while on tour with her production of Hélène Cixous' *Drums on the Dam* (1999), into the stories of Central Asian refugees and their lives in holding camps. Mnouchkine has integrated into her company as administrators, technicians, actors, and builders, political exiles from nearly every corner of the Earth, thus living the international camaraderie and understanding she promotes in her activism.

MNOUCHKINE IN THE 1980s AND BEYOND

The long-awaited victory of the French Left in the presidential elections of 1981 helped foreground the cultural importance of Ariane Mnouchkine and the artistic worth of the company. Socialist President François Mitterand named **Jack Lang** to head the Ministry of Culture, which meant for the arts in general, and for the Soleil in particular, a major boost in state subsidies. The Socialists, like all French rulers since at least Louis XIV, believed that investing in the arts would enhance France's prestige in the world. Lang accordingly doubled the Soleil's subvention to 4,000,000 francs. Today, the Théâtre du Soleil is the most heavily subsidized private theater company in France, although the members earn about the equivalency of a junior teacher's salary.

The government's largesse allowed the company to breathe a little easier: It no longer needed to resort to as many periods of unemployment benefits nor to selling tickets to loyal spectator/sponsors several months before productions began. The company was also increasingly invited to prestige international arts festival, to cite a few: **Avignon** (*Méphisto* 1980, *The Shakespeare Cycle* 1984, *Le Dernier Caravansérail* 2003); Jerusalem (*l'Indiade* 1988); the Brooklyn Academy of Music (*The House of Atreus Cycle* 1992); the Los Angeles Olympics' Arts Festival (*The Shakespeare Cycle* 1984); Lincoln Center (*Le Dernier Caravansérail* 2005). Since 1970, the Soleil has, in fact, been involved in major touring throughout Europe and North America. During 1992–3, for example, *The House of Atreus Cycle* went to Germany, Sicily, Canada, the Netherlands, and the United Kingdom, as well as the United States. With *Drums on the Dam*, the troupe took on a long tour of Asia, and traveled in Australia and New Zealand for almost a year (2001–2). Such movement meant, and will continue to necessitate, supervising and accommodating over fifty people and several tons of scenery and costumes for each production.

As much in political harmony as Mnouchkine may have felt during the relatively long tenure of the Socialist Party (until 1995), she did not let down her guard in terms of political scandal or international outrage. In 1994, for example, in an angry and contentious mood, she and author Hélène Cixous in their production, *The Perjured City*, gave dramatic form to the accusation against the government of trafficking in tainted blood. From 1980 on, she has, moreover, enlarged her concerns from the French sphere to a much larger geopolitical arena. Her productions have thus encompassed war-torn Cambodia (*Sihanouk* 1985); postcolonial India and Pakistan (*l'Indiade* 1987); and North Africa – in a redrafted *Tartuffe* (1995). This last production, with its warnings about Islamic fundamentalism, also hints at a France that can no longer be defined in outmoded nationalist and cultural terms. In *Le Dernier Caravansérail*, which continues the theme of exile found in *Et Soudain des nuits d'éveil*, Mnouchkine represents the slippery boundaries of refugees on the move. From Central Asia en route toward Europe and Australia, characters in *Le Dernier Caravansérail* display one of the prominent faces of humanity in the twenty-first century: the political and economic migrant.

Mnouchkine: spokesperson for cultural regeneration

Through the expansion of her subject materials, Mnouchkine indicates how in tune she is with the shifting contours of geopolitical reality. Her theater now re-situates France within a globalized network: Her questions no longer focus on the distance between social classes in a relatively comfortable world (*1789*), or even the integration of former colonized immigrants into a French context (*L'Age d'Or*), but rather on the unpredictable and uncontrollable flow of human beings from feuding, repressive, and transitioning regions into the so-called developed world. In *Le Dernier Caravansérail*, Mnouchkine even decenters what is most crucial to French identity, the French language. Actors speak in Farsi, Dari, and pidgin, while the play is supertitled in French. The make-up of the company reflects this widening geopolitical reach. As of 2005, there were seventy-five members from thirty-five countries, speaking twenty-two different languages. Of the company, at least five members have been saved from the refugee camps where Mnouchkine collected interviews for her *Caravansérail* production.

Mnouchkine situates her international company within her understanding of France today: "[Having] so many nationalities in the troupe comes from the fact that it is French theatre and thus a direct reflection of what France is now" (Féral 2001: 98). Mnouchkine's France, like her company, is cosmopolitan, open to a multitude of cultures, and unconstrained by aesthetic tradition. In this, she straddles a current divide in French political thinking. Unquestionably, in the camp of Republican France, committed to democracy, equality, and the separation of church and state, her work and her outlook are, nonetheless, inflected with the possibility of multiculturalism, even a sort of utopian inclusiveness. This is evident in the film she made with Hélène Cixous for French television in 1989 to celebrate the 200th anniversary of *The Declaration of the Rights of Man*. The film, *La Nuit miraculeuse*, in a kind of apotheosis of the progressive humanist dream, places delegates to the eighteenth-century

Revolutionary Assembly in conversation with Mahatma Gandhi, Martin Luther King, Jr, *hassidim*, disabled people, sign language interpreters, and many more representatives of particular social groups. Aware of the changing demographics and demands of recent immigrants who do not want to assimilate to "Frenchness" that is defined and naturalized as white, Christian, or European, Mnouchkine performs in recent pieces the tensions inherent not in the clash of cultures, but rather in the clash of fundamentalist nationalist and religious thinking. Her Théâtre du Soleil constitutes the kind of association of like-minded peoples that, since 1992, has largely replaced specific political parties in France.

THEATRICAL INFLUENCES AND AFFINITIES

Mnouchkine has mainly absorbed her training as a theater director through what she has read and what she has seen. This includes, especially throughout her adolescence, the great melodramatic novels of the nineteenth century: Hugo, Dickens, Verne, and Hardy, and the epic Japanese films of Kurosawa and Mizoguchi. She claims as her only masters the extraordinary experiences of seeing, as a girl, kathakali and **Balinese dancers** in Paris and, later, her 1962 pilgrimage to Asia, where she reveled in **bunraku**, **Noh**, and **kabuki**, among other performance styles: "Without knowing it, without even wanting it, I was amassing the treasure that would change my entire way of seeing, of living" (Pascaud 2005: 51).

With the notable and important exception of a year-long series of classes with Jacques Lecoq (1966–7), Mnouchkine has had little formal theater education. She became a director by directing. From her pungent discussions of theater, it is, however, clear that she has garnered vast personal resources from voracious readings in classics of the stage. Insatiably curious and entrepreneurial, she has also invited frequently, both in the cadre of the school she founded, ARTA, and outside of it, numerous international masters of theatrical and performance techniques to perform and run workshops at the Cartoucherie. Under ARTA's patronage and through the coordination of its co-directors Jean-François Dusigne and Lucia Bensasson, both former actors with the Soleil, professionals of kathakali, **Topeng**, Amerindian dancing, Indian martial arts, Chinese opera, and other traditional forms have been coming to the Cartoucherie four times a year for four-week stints since 1989. Mnouchkine has clearly profited from interactions with these professionals, as they have benefited from seeing her work. What has emerged as Mnouchkine's aesthetic in her productions since 1980 is a blending and reinterpretation of Asian techniques with the physical discipline and mask work she has always practiced. Her "style" is, consequently, very much her own, a theatrical language both transporting and empowering, but not easily reproducible.

MNOUCHKINE'S EUROPEAN GENEALOGY

Despite, or perhaps because of this mixing and interculturalism, we are able to suggest a European theatrical genealogy for Mnouchkine. To do so, we must return to the early part of the twentieth century – with its somewhat contradictory quests for new forms to achieve a sense of aesthetic transcendence and also new means to bring theater to society's less privileged. Mnouchkine can thus be placed within the double heritage of thinkers and practitioners such as Artaud (1896–1948), Craig (1872–1966), Meyerhold (1874–1940), and later Lecoq (1921–99), on the one hand – with their emphasis on formal experimentation – and, on the other, within the popular theater movement, especially the efforts of Jean Vilar (1912–71) and his commitment to theater as education. Jacques Copeau (1879–1949), with a foot in either camp, will become for Mnouchkine a kind of idealized mentor, someone she begins citing as early as 1975. She prefers, nonetheless, to classify herself and her generation as children of Jean Vilar, heeding his call to make theater a public service in order to secure the world's future: "We were born from that post-war spirit, those people who thought about peace after victory" (Pascaud 2005: 27).

"Primitivism," formal experimentation, and the search for theater

From the end of the nineteenth century, and in sync with a generalized European arts movement, part of the French art world has sought a way to uncover what the veneer of civilization has potentially hidden. To put this another way, many artists have hoped to re-find the soul of art they believed buried by bourgeois and industrialized society. Some perceived this soul in what was considered to be "primitive" art from non-Western countries. The opening of the Far East to trade and the colonial conquests of major European powers brought cultural forms to Paris that were to have a profound impact on arts practitioners. For example, the 1900 Universal Exposition in Paris focused attention on the Japanese performer Sadda Yacco, whose kabuki-inspired movements suggested a whole other way of performing in space, a means of inscribing emotion and meaning through focusing energy and attention on the body. Searching for "reality" beyond the commitment to reason and logic, which the **Enlightenment** project had privileged, suspicious of the construction of a real which did not include dream states and intuition, theater-makers pursued contact with arts from Asia as a means of inventing a theater both multi-layered and emotionally truthful.

Antonin Artaud, once considered a holy pariah and now the best-known among those artists enthralled by the Paris-based Colonial Exposition of 1931, interpreted the Balinese dancers he saw there as possessing the secret of what theater had to become if it were to be true again: emotionally contagious, physically communicative, even ecstatic, and estranging – that is, liberating the actor and the spectator from quotidian reality. His essays, collected in *The Theatre and Its Double* (1938, translated into English in 1958), found a receptive audience among major experimental theater people in the 1960s. Directors such as **Peter Brook** and **Jerzy Grotowski**, in their respective laboratory theaters in London and Wroclaw, developed approaches to making theater that incorporated Artaud's stress on the actor as a medium and that, under Artaudian promptings, placed the dark side of the human psyche onstage.

Although Mnouchkine only began to read Artaud after several years of doing theater and has never claimed him as a source, we can find Artaudian echoes throughout her work, as, indeed, throughout the experimental work of countless companies formed in the 1960s and 1970s. To cite the most obvious, we note parallels between Artaud's emphasis on sensory stimulation in order to engage fully one's public with Mnouchkine's kaleidoscopic use of music, color, lighting, and movement: This is constant throughout her *mises-en-scène*. Moreover, Artaud's exhilarating and confounding writings underlie and bolster theoretically her move away from textual centeredness to performances that take their meaning notably through gesture, sound, and spatial configurations. Mnouchkine has flirted with bracketing texts and giving them secondary status during her entire career. She has also refined her physical work to promote a kind of actor-athlete-dancer reminiscent of Artaud's "athlete of the heart" (see Figure 1.1).

Figure 1.1 Choral dancing by members of the Théâtre du Soleil inspired by *bharata natyam* work, for *The House of Atreus Cycle*; here Aeschylus's *The Libation Bearers*, 1991

Mnouchkine's stunningly fit and balletic actors are not without recalling Edward Gordon Craig's fascination with the marionette – an iconic form intriguing to Artaud, as well. What better vehicle for exteriorizing psychic states and focusing on myths and magic, for reinforcing a ritualistic pattern of performance, for taking distance from the everyday, for heightening the sense of "presentness?" Mnouchkine's work with actors, especially since *The Shakespeare Cycle* (1990–2), would seem to realize a dream of theater evoked by the multitalented director Craig, in which the focus on discipline and performance prevents the actors' egos from permeating the characters. Actors become, instead, part of a semiotic language wherein space, volume, lights, symbolic movements, and music are the central sense-givers. Like Craig, Mnouchkine would evacuate domesticated acting conventions to install creation and invention in their place. She would go after "universal" meaning rather than portray individual psychological trauma.

In her emphasis on light and shadow, on mass and absence, we also see suggestions of the expressionist films Mnouchkine so loved as a child. We might also locate here certain affinities with Vsevolod Meyerhold's principles of biomechanics – a coded system of movements and gestures meant to elicit certain specific emotional reactions from the public. Mnouchkine, indeed, acknowledges a certain interest in Meyerhold's theories, taking inspiration not only from his physical work but also in *1789* from his thoughts on street theater production and in *Le Dernier Caravansérail* from his use of glides and stage wagons.

Of this associative genealogy, the only person with whom Mnouchkine actually worked and whose training, as mentioned earlier, she carried back in the evenings to sessions with her own actors during rehearsals for *The Kitchen* (1966–7) was Jacques Lecoq. She credits him with being a major modern influence in re-situating theater within the actor's body:

> More than anyone else, Lecoq understood what a body was all about. Before he taught in France, very many [theatre] people still believed that an actor's only instruments were memory, voice, and words.
>
> (Pascaud 2005: 25)

More of a teacher than a theoretician or practitioner, Lecoq, from his school in Paris (1956–99), has oriented the work of some of the most important theater artists and companies of contemporary times, including

Théâtre de Complicité in the United Kingdom. Mnouchkine would seem to have borrowed from Lecoq a training vocabulary used consistently in her workshops and rehearsals (e.g. "corporeal writing," "playing *v.* interpreting," a "state" – or the character's on-stage emotional being; see the section titled, "A basic rehearsal vocabulary" in Chapter 4). She has also adopted his passion for improvised mask work. Her commitment to group improvisations and to involving all actors in the process of seeing and selecting are also techniques we can locate in Lecoq's training repertory.

Unlike Lecoq, Mnouchkine has never trained her actors in neutral masks, finding rather, in the *commedia dell'arte* forms she studied with him in the late 1960s, or in the Balinese forms adopted later on, a better approximation, from the outset, for the models of the modern human comedy she has always sought to create. Individuated masks are also, she feels, a better prompt for the narratives she builds: *Commedia* masks in particular make evident the truths about life that people do not readily see. Reverberations of what can be thought of as Lecoq's universe can be gleaned most clearly in early Soleil productions: *1789* and *l'Age d'Or*, most particularly – especially in the latter's elaborate mask work, in which actors developed modern characters (an immigrant construction worker, a capitalist, a feminist) on frames of Harlequin, Pantaloon, and Pulchinello.

Theater as public service and educational tool

Theater's impetus to instruct is as old as theater itself, an impetus, however, frequently taking a backseat to entertainment. At the beginning of the twentieth century, French theater-makers from political and educational backgrounds sought to wrest theater from what was considered to be the dominant production mode: self-involved and superficial *divertissement* – vaudevilles, triangular trysts, and operettas. Moreover, this theater targeted only one kind of spectator: someone with the leisure time and money to be able to afford an evening out.

Ideologically oriented theater-makers, such as the pacifist Romain Rolland, endeavored as early as 1907 to bring theater to "the people" as a way of including the working classes in the artistic celebrations of French culture and identity. This strand of support for what was called "popular theater" led, eventually, to the creation of the first Théâtre National Populaire (1920) in an effort to help build the nation by democratizing culture. Later championed by the government of the Popular Front in 1936, the popular theater movement culminated in two related actions: the reincarnation in 1951 of the Théâtre National Populaire under Jean Vilar in Paris' Palais de Chaillot, and the post-war push for **decentralized** and subsidized theaters and *maisons de la culture* throughout France.

Vilar devoted his considerable talents to creating a theater that would bring both the greatest theater classics and the best new theater to a broad swathe of France's population. To achieve this result, he practiced reduced prices, close cooperation with union-affiliated cultural committees in various factories, inexpensive meals in the theater itself, programs which also included theater texts, and talk backs with actors and directors. He expanded the reach of his work by initiating, with the help of local Provençal political authorities, the Avignon Theater Festival – a remarkably successful move that, since its inception in 1947, has helped ballast the project to create subsidized theaters throughout the French provinces.

Growing up in the effervescence of Vilar's passion and artistic benchmarks, Mnouchkine inherited from him a blueprint on how to best reach non-elite audiences. She also claimed for her own Vilar's effort to make theater part of every citizen's right to culture as well as his dedication to theater as part of a national conversation. Mnouchkine had always admired Vilar and the feeling was mutual: He even considered her a promising candidate to direct, after his retirement, the Avignon Festival. His was, however, a theater of reconciliation. As Mnouchkine developed, faithful, too, to her generation and its enthusiasm for the Brechtian-inspired and influential theater review, *Théâtre Populaire* (1953–64), she leaned, at least in the first phase of her work, toward a more overtly politicized theater, one that would hold up to inspection the capitalist system, one that would involve "the people" in its creation.

In addition to incorporating in her institutional practice many of Vilar's techniques for building new audiences, Mnouchkine has also, like Vilar, revisited from time to time great classics of the Western theater, recasting them in light of the contemporary scene (*The Shakespeare Cycle, The House of Atreus Cycle, Tartuffe*). Mnouchkine and Vilar intersect also in the use of a vast, empty playing space in which the geography of the staging and the physical virtuosity of the actors bear the weight of meaning. In this latter similarity, we also see the shadow of

Jacques Copeau, whose vision of theater has been, to a certain extent, realized in the work of Ariane Mnouchkine. He, too, before Vilar and before Mnouchkine, invented a fixed theatrical space that in its emptiness could become the site of all possibilities. And in the short run of his innovative Vieux Columbier (1913–14), and his long experimental phase in the Burgundian countryside (1924–36), he was able to put into practice exercises for creating a modern *commedia dell'arte* form.

Part of the group of innovative artists and intellectuals connected to the literary review *La Nouvelle Review Française (NRF)*, Copeau, and Copellian ideas, have played since 1910 a central role in orienting the direction of French theater – and this despite how frequently his own career was interrupted by the vicissitudes of war and politics. His disciples and students have included such noted interwar directors as **Charles Dullin** and **Louis Jouvet**. His descendants – relatives, such as Jean Dasté and spiritual sons, such as Jean-Marie Serreau – have been mainstays in the decentralization movement, a movement Copeau foresaw in his Burgundian workshops in the 1920s. Indeed, today there is a remarkable family of theater workers, all in some way descended from Copeau – still administering, acting, and directing in decentralized theaters throughout France.

With the *NRF* team, adepts of the **modernist** spirit, Copeau sought to make the arts a means for transcendent understanding and pleasure, a principle key to discovering cultural "others," including the others inside each human being. His project was visionary, featuring the creation of a fellowship of actors dedicated to working together – exquisitely physically trained in order to build collectively a new, modern comedy with symbolic characters capturing the major conflicts of the times. Copeau's central position as director and guru shored up the role of the theatrical director in France and helped pave the way for the kind of director's theater that has emerged since the 1970s. Mnouchkine fits into these patterns while inflecting them. Fiercely committed to theater work which grapples with the most urgent social and political questions, she also will not work without a collective. But Mnouchkine is much less the guru than was Copeau. She connects symbiotically with her actors. Nevertheless, her collective would not exist without her authority: She is not only the sole theater director, but also both the artistic and administrative director, involved in all processes of decision-making at all levels.

MNOUCHKINE, CONTEMPORARY FRENCH THEATER, AND VISIONARY PEERS

It is not an exaggeration to say that of the several flourishing art forms in France, theater has been especially crucial since the Second World War to the country's understanding of itself and articulation of its values. The extraordinary formal experimentation that took hold of the French theater world in the 1950s expressed as well as anything the existential anguish of the post-war period and demonstrated France's fecund reception of exiled or wandering artists and intellectuals. Almost simultaneously, Brecht and Brechtian theatrical ideals found enthusiastic audiences and adepts for political speculation and activism in order to promote democracy and reign in capitalist expansion. The several new venues for broadening notions of what theater might be – the Théâtre des Nations (1957–75), The Festival d'Automne (1972–), the Théâtre de l'Europe (1981–) – have welcomed companies from around the world and have had a profound impact within France on intercultural collaboration, multicultural perspectives, and the modeling of what a fully integrated European cultural and political scene might be.

At the beginning of the twenty-first century, theater in France is still thriving, grandly supported by state coffers in the provinces as well as in Paris, well represented in prestigious international festival circuits, and newly claiming a place as a disciplinary concentration for secondary students. The debate launched by Director Antoine Vitez in the 1980s on just what constitutes theater has also pitted directors against authors against actors, choreographers, and devisors, as each stretches conventions and attempts to posit new rules for what makes up a theatrical text, a theatrical performer, or a theatrical act. Meanwhile, the intellectual passion for "theatricality" as a concept has led to myriad meditations on performance and performativity as the only ways of grasping reality. Theater as material construction has thus given way in some circles to "theater" as a set of structures for understanding communication.

Within these debates and experimentations, Mnouchkine has remained remarkably true to her earliest sense of theater as a service to a community – a forum for justice but also a reconnection to the universe. Hers has always been a dual commitment to regenerate theater and society, while the "masked bodies" of her actors have signaled a genuine breakthrough in the development of Western performance practice, the culmination of something desired but never fully realized by Artaud and Copeau. Through her focus on actors and her penchant for theatrical allegory, she has broken completely with the remnants of European theater's dependency on realism, privileging a total theater experience. She also continues to feed an immense ambition which is no less than to capture the world by fleshing out in metaphorical form patterns of struggle that mark our times. Consequently, her work, as discussed earlier, has evolved thematically and structurally in response to the acute crisis of identity experienced by France and, beyond that, by human communities caught in the shifting tides of new geopolitics.

No one in France is working as Ariane Mnouchkine does today. Of the older generation, Peter Brook, who shares her intercultural interests, has reduced the scope of his productions. Her much admired contemporary, **Patrice Chéreau**, who shares an aesthetic of trembling intensity, has turned primarily to film and opera. Among women directors, only Brigitte Jacque-Wadjman has run a grand scale theatrical institution.

Mnouchkine can indeed be linked to Peter Brook in terms of the inter and transcultural experimentation she undertakes, in terms of her multicultural company, and in terms of the mythic opulence of her productions. Brook's work, however, has a mystical edge that keeps it hovering, in most cases, beyond the immediately political. Of the younger generation of international directors whose work bears comparison with Mnouchkine – either because of its scope, its creative impetus and history, or its visual excitement – most, such as **Robert Lepage**, **Simon McBurney**, and Peter Sellars, are more theoretically anchored and technologically savvy. While incorporating video and mixed media, they tend to ask how humans construct the real, whereas Mnouchkine has largely abandoned since the 1980s the option of multiple perspectives and the play between representation and reality. Hers is a theater now incorporating elements of epic storytelling and dance theater, with the actor as linchpin of the experience, pushed to his or her creative acme through the kind of collective thinking and working Mnouchkine requires and extols.

It is difficult to ascribe to Mnouchkine any direct artistic descendants, especially if we exclude Philippe Caubère, who has made his career by parodying her in cabaret numbers, or other Soleil actors, notably Jean-Claude Penchenat, who, upon leaving the Soleil have created their own companies inevitably colored by their experience with Mnouchkine.

Mnouchkine's aura is too huge, her achievements too great, her originality too complex to give birth to in any kind of obvious manner younger artists. Her legacy, however, will continue to permeate the spirit of theatrical production not only in France but also throughout the world. As citizen-artist, she will be known for keeping history theatrically alive for public and company members alike in a conscious process of witnessing and debating. As aesthetic experimenter, she will be celebrated for incessant and untiring exploration, blending, and invention of theatrical forms – from clowning to cabaret, from *commedia dell'arte* to Asian martial arts and ritualized performance traditions. As company leader and institutional innovator, she will be admired for creating a joyful, if demanding, communal – even tribal – experience where, as she puts it, you can "have your friends and your lovers in the same place and you can still be a nomad" (Pascaud 2005: 9).

2

IDEAS ON THEATER

Theater as collective history and the quest for form

Theatre is a place of language and of thought, an exploration of the facts and the soul of history. [. . .] Theatre is still a place where one learns, where one tries to understand, where one is moved, where one encounters the Other and where one becomes other.

(Féral 1998: 15)

Ariane Mnouchkine, despite her claims of not being a theoretician, has accorded over the past thirty-five years a series of judicious and substantive interviews about her work from which we can readily discern what theater means to her. As in the quote that introduces this chapter, she enumerates consistently her sense of what theater must do. It must confront history in an attempt to understand history's impact on both the individual and the collective life. It must move people metaphorically out of their own skins in order to transform them – not only through an encounter with human others but also through meeting the others within oneself.

In confident terms, Ariane Mnouchkine also speaks of her belief in what theater must be: "I believe in wonder. I believe in stimulation through beauty, light, hope, joy, laughter, tears" (Féral 1998: 16). In other words, for Ariane Mnouchkine theater must be an emotionally energizing voyage. It must also be beautiful. Above all, it must be a learning process, a form of modern day quest.

In the 1970 and 1980 interviews compiled by David Williams in *Collaborative Theatre* as well as in her answers to Josette Féral's 1998 queries in *Trajectoires du Soleil: autour d'Ariane Mnouchkine*, Mnouchkine has especially insisted on the open-endedness of her process. She has also been brutally frank about its difficulties. In speaking about the crisis in the collective writing of *l'Age d'Or* (1974), for example, she worries:

> I do not see why one only has the right to be called an author if one has a pen. An improvising actor is an author, an author in the broadest sense of the term. So we have authors. But the problem is that we are very much novices in this practice.

> (Williams 1999: 55)

Not only does she worry about failure in authorship, but she also worries about failure of imagination. In musing about her stalled attempt to imagine with author Hélène Cixous a play based on the French Resistance (1998–9), she admits:

> The very essence of Resistance is to act in the dark. [...] Theatre is the art of light, it's a bringing into light – and for the moment, I can't figure out how I'm going to light what is dark.

> (Féral 1998: 36)

This image of lighting what is dark captures Ariane Mnouchkine's directorial project. By figuring out, imagining, and reinventing new forms for interrogations of history and of political life, and by redefining what a collective theater process can be she makes each production of the Théâtre du Soleil the latest stage of a work in progress.

In this chapter, we will explore the why and the how of this work in progress by turning most often to Williams' and Féral's excellent collections of interviews and commentaries. We will see that while Mnouchkine's emphasis on what is most important in theater work has somewhat changed, she has nevertheless remained strikingly focused on the idea of ongoing pedagogical research. We should also keep in mind that Mnouchkine's quest has always been inclusive: of the actors, technicians, and other artists of the Théâtre du Soleil, as well as of the spectators. Mnouchkine does not think or create outside of the collective sphere.

THEORETICAL PROPOSITIONS

THEATER AS ENGAGEMENT WITH HISTORY

Since her early ventures with the Théâtre du Soleil, Ariane Mnouchkine has declared history to be central to her theatrical concerns. She has puzzled over how best to represent it. She has worried over which history to represent. She has especially committed herself to directing productions that encourage her spectators to situate themselves within the historical process. She believes that if spectators can see themselves as part of a system, then they will also be able to see that history can be changed and acted upon.

This latter notion helps us understand how Mnouchkine tends to define history, because "history" can be a slippery and complicated category of knowledge. For Mnouchkine, "history" means more than past events. It connotes, rather, a narrative of events that are thought to have altered the direction of contemporary societies and nations. History, in this light, is never distant from the present. Past and present reflect dialectically upon each other. Thus in Mnouchkine's work, she always connects what has happened – and how this has been interpreted – with what is happening. Furthermore, she often focuses on what she deems to be history in the making – or contemporary events of such import that they are sure to have an impact on how society and the individuals who compose it move and change. Concentrating on "history," as just presented, provides Mnouchkine with a rich source for political commentary.

In the course of the Théâtre du Soleil's 1970–2 elaboration of its now legendary collective reinterpretation of the French Revolution (*1789* and *1793*), Mnouchkine frequently invoked the need to tell a story about history with which every audience, and particularly a popular audience, could engage. She began then to articulate her sense of history as the spine of her work:

> [We] realized that the only heritage common to all French people, even if it is distorted, is the History of France. We wanted to create a work on a subject that everyone would feel they knew. The "spine" emerged from this desire.

> (Williams 1999: 17)

Her desire to reel in spectators through a story that spoke to their identity as subjects in history has, indeed, underscored her choice not only of plays and topics, but also of key staging patterns. She has based her creative process in part on how best to include spectators in historical representation.

At its most obvious, Mnouchkine's commitment to history can be heard in the pressing and timely themes that orient her shows: for example, the exploitation of immigrant workers (*l'Age d'Or*, 1975–6); the operation of totalitarian thought (*Méphisto*, 1979–80); the imposition of foreign ideologies on indigenous governing structures (*The Terrible but Unfinished Tragedy of Norodom Sihanouk, King of Cambodia*, 1985–6); the struggle for individuation within a communal power base (Euripides and Aeschylus: *The House of Atreus Cycle*, 1990–2); or the horror of refugee life (*Le Dernier Caravansérail*, 2003). These themes constitute a gamut of problems that, together, provide a reading of contemporary history in the making. Whether collectively created (*1789, 1793, l'Age d'Or, Et soudain des nuits d'éveil* (1997), and *Le Dernier Caravansérail*); or scripted (*The Shakespeare Cycle* (1981–4), *The House of Atreus Cycle*, and *Tartuffe* (1995–6)); or written expressly for the Soleil (Mnouchkine's own adaptation of Thomas Mann's *Méphisto* and Hélène Cixous's four modern epics), the productions that Mnouchkine has initiated, developed, and brought to fruition since 1970 have all grappled with events or incidents considered central in the formation of contemporary sociopolitical structures. In certain cases, such as her reading of Moliere's *Tartuffe* as a parable of Islamic fundamentalism, she has reinterpreted stories to be politically meaningful in a modern historical context.

The first phase: history and militancy

In what can be called a first, overtly politicized phase (1970–80), Mnouchkine did not hesitate to take a Marxist approach to conceptualizing history. History in works of this period can be understood as the story of class struggle and rampant capitalism. Throughout her work on *1789, 1793, l'Age d'Or*, and *Méphisto*, she created works of denunciation, accusation, and demonstration. To schematize, all four productions were focused in such a way as to show the bad faith of the bourgeois power structure and its exclusive hunger for material rewards. On the other hand, the working class, even if shown as clever in these productions, is ultimately blocked by a system that privileges the rich.

These early productions were designed to involve the audience in the physical action of the performance, each one establishing a different and compelling rapport between public and playing space. For example, for *l'Age d'Or* – a series of **commedia dell'arte** sketches meant to encapsulate power struggles in work and domestic spheres – audience members followed the actors up and down the four craters comprising the "stage." They labored to keep up with the pace of the movement and were included in what became a kind of improvised blocking. In *Méphisto* – which opposed a Marxist ideology to a fascist one – spectators had to switch their chair backs around 180 degrees every time the stage action moved from one end of the playing space to the other. In these Artaudian – like configurations, they became the audience of either the communist cabaret or the bourgeois repertory theater situated at opposite ends of the theater space. Mnouchkine believed that this physical participation would strengthen the audience's adhesion to her plays' messages of struggle, protest, and enlightenment.

Mnouchkine's desire to interact intimately with her spectators, so as to keep them aware of their own potential for action, also led her to make the audience part of the creative process. This effort – echoed in the work of a number of radicalized French companies of the 1960s and 1970s – brought culturally disenfranchised people to the theater and encouraged them to partake in theater-making. For *l'Age d'Or*, this meant performing sketches before a rural public or bringing in workers to rehearsals to comment on scenes:

> [We] have tried to get workers from particular factories, groups of nurses or soldiers to come tell us not what we already know about them – in other words, what one reads in any of the left-wing newspapers – but what we don't know.
>
> (Williams 1999: 53–4)

Mnouchkine thus sought to learn from those people often neglected by official history. Their reactions became part of the collective vision of the production.

In these early efforts at capturing history onstage – including history in progress – Mnouchkine thought of the actor, as well, as responsible for elaborating the theatrical text. With Mnouchkine as a partner but undoubtedly "first among equals," Soleil actors collectively devised theater texts that would never be termed "finished," as with *l'Age d'Or*, subtitled "*The First Draft*." Collaborating through collective scripting allowed the actors to feel as though they, too, were participating in the process of revisiting history, of analyzing it according to their own political understanding. Louis Samier says this clearly in characterizing his participation in *1789*:

> Not only do I feel like an actor here, but I find myself in tune with what I'm making and what I'm making is myself [...] in performance and outside of it. I can't imagine a professional future anywhere else, because I can no longer imagine working in "the profession" as it's usually understood.
>
> (Williams 1999: 30)

The actors' creative work thus became the expression of their political identity.

In this first phase of Mnouchkine's career, the Théâtre du Soleil came closest to realizing the expressed goal of turning theater-making into a communal paradise. The theater world of the Soleil blurred the barrier between art and life, between being a creative force and an informed, even militant, citizen. In this, the Soleil also reflected what had become possible and desirable for artistic communities in the immediate wake of "The Events of May 68" and in the restless political climate of the 1960s and 1970s. Engaging with history through theater meant direct and immediate confrontation with illegitimate power in a carnivalesque and self-conscious style. The Soleil (i.e. Mnouchkine, actors, technicians, and even to a large extent their audience) formed an engaged collectivity committed to radically questioning how interpretations of history had been used to bolster undemocratic structures, or how such structures were currently being allowed to evolve.

The second phase: history as allegory and excavation

In the second, more sustained phase of her research (from 1980 and the Shakespeare project: *Richard II*, *Twelfth Night*, and *Henry IV, Part I* to *Le Dernier Caravansérail*, 2003), Mnouchkine's approach to history has been more oblique and less preoccupied with immediately stirring up her public. Indeed, she has changed the form of her performance space in such a way as to put some physical distance between audience and actors. While the spectators sit on bleachers, the performers play on a vast open platform facing – and sometimes extending under – the bleachers. This has established a fixed and more contemplative rapport between the audience and the actors. Performance now calls for rapt attention and instills in the public the sense of attending an often shattering ritual – for the Soleil's more recent productions body forth trauma, genocide, political corruption, and the lust for power.

Hélène Cixous, company author since 1984, describes the shift in Mnouchkine's thinking about engaging with history in this way:

> We dream of telling in such a way that something will move in reality. If not change – which would be enormously presumptuous – then at least be recalled, resuscitated, delivered from silence [...] an illumination of the present itself.
>
> (Prenowitz 2004: 27)

Mnouchkine now focuses on theatrical acts that uncover those scandalous situations endangering the future of a just world. Engaging with history connotes selecting or initiating epic texts which have the kind of metaphorical thickness that allow them to be read as parables of unhealthy contemporary political structures. *Richard II* (1980), for example, a Shakespearian history play based on regime change during the reign of the Plantagenets, was also meant to be read in Mnouchkine's production as a demonstration of how power passes from ruler to ruler, bypassing the citizenry. Cixous' *l'Indiade ou l'Inde de leurs rêves* (1987–8) gives shape to the history of the partition of the Indian subcontinent, but should also be understood as portraying the brutal results of the claims of ethnic identity against nationhood. Her *Drums on the Dam*, in the form of an ancient puppet play, performed by actors (1999–2000), while imaging a medieval Chinese ruler's destruction of his own people, also posits the grave danger of unilateral power that ends up destroying itself as well as others. The contemporary reference in all these readings is inescapable. In originating and directing these works, Mnouchkine asks questions about ethics, rather than skewering a particular economic hegemony, as she did through her earlier, more Marxist-influenced approach. She is bent on making theater which exposes the barbarism of today's world and which critiques what she perceives as a contaminating ethical void. Discussing Cixous' *The Perjured City* (1994), which pointedly attacks the French government officials and medical people who did not stop the transfusion of HIV-infected blood to over 2,000 hemophiliacs, Mnouchkine restated the ethical crux of her research: "I think that the story of the blood – this crime – is absolutely the metaphor for our society. [. . .] What is our morality? Or, rather, what's the meaning of this absence of morality?" (Shevtsova 1995: 70). It is with the gravitas of this question that she installed *Le Dernier Caravansérail* in her theater, "born of a need to protect against pillage" (program notes 2003); that is, erected to honor and give voice and shape to the stories of Afghan, Kurdish, and other Central Asian refugees who have passed from one site of terror to another.

The shift in Mnouchkine's engagement with history has engendered a concomitant shift in the way in which she wishes to connect with the public. We have mentioned the change in spatial design that blunts active physical participation. Mnouchkine has also rethought what and how she wants her characters to be. She has made a very conscious theoretical and performance choice to distance the tone and feel of her pieces from the Soleil's earlier, more satirical works. Mnouchkine is now convinced that by representing onstage some configuration of "the stranger," or "the other," she will force the public to really look and listen. The psychic attachment to a symbolic other self, aesthetically distanced from the everyday, will be, she believes, profound and jolting. Hence, she purposely makes the characters strange, such as the **hyper-real**, almost cartoon-like, Indian people of *l'Indiade*, or the expressionistic homeless chorus of *The Perjured City*, or the broadly drawn Central Asian refugees in *Le Dernier Caravansérail*. Through location (Cambodia, Cixous' *Sihanouk*), through situation (dead children, *The Perjured City*), through performance (**kathakali**-inspired figures, *The House of Atreus Cycle*, or humanoid puppets, *Drums on the Dam*), or through a combination of these and other alienating, or strange-making techniques, Mnouchkine makes the audience work harder in order to feel with and experience the often tragic circumstances of "the other." For Mnouchkine, this deep and complex emotional knowledge, affected through a kind of troubled identification, empowers her public.

Quite early in her career, Mnouchkine told the theater historian and critic Denis Bablet, "**Brecht** is not a form, it's a vision of theatre" (Williams 1999: 56). She has undoubtedly absorbed Brecht's vision, or at least that part of the vision that sees theater as playing a major role in educating citizens to the social and political structures that help determine how history gets made. What has manifestly changed in Mnouchkine's approach to history is her sense of the proper form to achieve her ends.

She has evolved in her thinking from the necessity for a direct, action-based and action-oriented theater, emerging in part out of a close rapport between actor/creators and potential audience members, to a call for a responsible theater of dense and legendary epic texts which allegorize the powerful constraints governing life in contemporary society.

THEATER AS TRANSCENDENT AND TRANSFORMATIVE

It was in the second phase of her research, and especially during her much heralded direction of *The Shakespeare Cycle* (1980–4), that Ariane Mnouchkine began to articulate an idea of theater that holds sway in all her interviews since then. Theater must be, above all else, theatrical. She firmly believes that "survival consists in putting into theatre what can only exist in the theatre" (Williams 1999: 95). One way of understanding Mnouchkine's quest for a "theatrical theater," something we might also call "true theater," is to embrace the idea that theater for her becomes a means of digging more deeply into life. Indeed, theater should take us to the life obscured by everyday reality. She tells us: "Shakespeare is not our contemporary, and shouldn't be treated as such. He is as far from us as our own profoundest depths are far from us" (Williams 1999: 93). "True theater" must arrive at these depths – which, in some of Mnouchkine's pronouncements sound more like heights. Thus, she intimates, theater moves us to a transcendent realm, to an undefined but felt metaphysical space, a place that holds life's forces rather than displaying the products of a materialist culture.

The idea of "theatrical theater" does not exactly contradict the importance of history as the foundation of her work. But it does suggest how she will begin to focus especially on formal investigation, how she will prioritize the physical and the visual. From 1980 on, we will hear her speak of a vision of theater that recalls more pointedly Artaud's quasi-mystical aesthetic rather than a Brechtian commitment to political revolution. Nonetheless, it should be noted that the attraction to beauty that this vision entails – to highly stylized forms, awe-inspiring materials, oversized and majestic costumes, precision choreography and music, radiant colors, and warm lighting – was definitely present in her earliest *mises-en-scène*.

In looking for "true theater," Mnouchkine will concentrate on discovering what she calls the theatrical laws that underpin many of the great classical and ceremonious traditions: *commedia dell'arte*, Shakespearian tragedies, Greek tragedies, Japanese **Noh** and **kabuki**. She will rail against the "venom of psychological realism" (Williams 1999: 94) that has infected and deformed the theatrical experience. Realism (cause and effect logic, exacting material replication, and "psychologizing"), she says, have crept into theater from cinema and television and have flattened and diminished it. A realist aesthetic tends to confirm rather than disturb what people already know about themselves. Mnouchkine will instead seek a challenging, barely recognizable form as a means of transporting the audience to a higher plane of feeling and knowing.

The crucial role of the director and of the actors is to find this form – one which will peel off the layers of familiarity that keep humans from seeing what life really is:

> [The theatre artist] goes into a tunnel that's very long, very deep, very strange, very dark at times and, [...] like a miner, brings back pebbles. [...] The first part of the adventure is to descend into the soul of beings, of a society, and then to return. The second part is the cutting of the diamonds without shattering them, finding the original form of the diamond in the pebble.
>
> (Williams 1999: 118)

This quest is fatiguing and riddled with wrong turns – with smashed pebbles instead of perfect diamonds – but, Mnouchkine suggests, it is the only possible way of restoring greatness to the theater and of restoring theater to life.

Musing over her recent work with Mnouchkine, Hélène Cixous defines their theatrical arena as multiform, as being at the same time the realm of the unconscious, of the spiritual, and the political. Within this space, "gods" travel freely:

> There is no theatre without gods. [...] God is what I would call all the superior forces with which we negotiate or which treat or mistreat us, which we imagine at times to be interior, but which we experience as exterior.
>
> (Prenowitz 2004: 5)

In Mnouchkine's and Cixous's works, the echoes of Antonin Artaud reverberate: Theater is more vital, more urgent than everyday life. It is a potent strategy for deciphering, or at least looking in the eyes, the "gods" that haunt us. It is a space of psychic danger and liberation.

Mask work and the Asian turn

To arrive at theater's potential for transcendence and transformation, Mnouchkine has chosen two challenging and interrelated routes: basing characters in mask work and using Asian theatrical practices to enrich approaches to movement, to costume, and to overall texture. In Mnouchkine's fervent dedication to masks, we see the lasting effect of her schooling with Jacques Lecoq. In her fascination with Asia, we see her commitment to experiment with de-familiarizing forms. We also see, in her experimentation with Japanese Noh, kabuki, and **bunraku**, and with Indian kathakali and **bharata natyam**, how she participates in a more generalized intercultural turn. Interculturalism, or the interest in and integration of other than one's own cultural art forms, has recently marked the work of such noted theater practitioners as **Peter Brook** and **Eugenio Barba**. It is explained by critic Patrice Pavis as theater's need to fill a vacuum in meaning – after the failure of more highly politicized theater to account for contemporary life (Pavis 1992). Turning to Asia for formal inspiration may well be seen as an attempt to find an integrative model of experience, one more relevant to today's geopolitics. Mnouchkine, however, expresses her interest in Asian theater in another way, which again foregrounds her notion of a universal theatrical form: "We look for a basis for our work in Asian theatre because that's where the very origin of theatrical form is" (Williams 1999: 93). For Mnouchkine, Asian theater, and the mask work inherent in it, proposes through stylization the kind of aesthetic shock which grabs the sinews and the minds of the audience.

Because the mask is understood by Mnouchkine as a site of transformation, mask work grounds the basis of the training she offers in her workshops and, consequently, determines how she expects her actors to handle the stage during rehearsals and performance. Even her unmasked actors, as in *The Perjured City*, must act as though masked. And while she will not always use the wooden or leather masks so salient in *l'Age d'Or*, *Richard II*, or *Sihanouk*, in later shows, stunning and intricate make-up, as in *l'Indiade* or the four-part *House of Atreus Cycle*, function like masks. In *Le Dernier Caravansérail*, we might even posit that the languages spoken by the actors (Farsi, Kurdish, Dari) realize a form of mask.

Mnouchkine works with two kinds of masks: *commedia dell'arte* and **Balinese** (or **Topeng**) forms. Both types of mask force her, she believes, to make a direct connection to how theater works: "With masks, all the laws of theatre come together. You can't get away from them" (Féral 1998: 29). Philippe Caubère, who created the role of Abdallah in *l'Age d'Or* (see Figure 2.1), explains how working with the Harlequin mask under the watchful eye of Mnouchkine conveyed the laws of mask work, and thus of theater, to him:

> [I understood] that the psychological characteristics could only be of use to me if I transposed them into theatrical signs. To get the maximum impact, [I found that] I should freeze the outline of body and mask in space for a fraction of a second: In this way I would give the audience the time to receive the images, to understand them and to laugh at them.
>
> (Williams 1999: 71)

Restating Caubère's discovery, Mnouchkine submits that working correctly with masks allows bodies to become forms, figures, and signs – or easily readable visual images. Masks help actors develop a set of coded gestures so as to be able to write in space. Masks demand that actors invent the details that give them life. Mask work guides the audience so that it identifies with the emotion that is given shape through movement. Masks thus deflect the kind of identification with facial expression prevalent in the realist tradition.

Mnouchkine feels that in permitting the mask to come alive through his or her body, the actor is also transported, becoming a kind of divine presence. In mask work, actors are required to renounce their egos, lose their self-consciousness and give up the boundaries that anchor them in place, time, and class. They liberate themselves from the markers of Western identity. Thus not only do "masked" actors strengthen the sense of ritual in a Mnouchkine production, but by the prodigious physical displays necessitated by the integration of masks, they become ciphers to another emotional sphere. In *The House of Atreus Cycle*, for example, the shaking, convulsing bodies of the chorus transmitted to the public the emotional impact of the play's horrific actions: infanticide (*Iphigenia*), parricide (*Agamemnon*), matricide (*The Libation Bearers*), vengeance (*The Eumenides*). Choral members physically delineated, in a promise of catharsis, the illness of the soul that permeates the story of the Atreus line.

Mnouchkine speaks of theater as "another continent" (Williams 1999: 166). What better way for a European theater practitioner to travel to this other continent than by incorporating and simulating the actual other continent of Asia? Mnouchkine's Asia must, however, be

Figure 2.1 The actor Philippe Caubère, in a Harlequin mask, as Abdallah the immigrant construction worker, *l'Age d'Or*, 1975

understood as a fantasy of Asia – just as her use of a kabuki-like stage
and kabuki movements in *Richard II*, bharata natyam hand and feet gestures in *Twelfth Night*, kutiyattam and kathakali dance and make-up in
the *The House of Atreus Cycle*, or bunraku puppets in *Drums on the Dam*, as
well as her portrayal of India in *l'Indiade*, must be seen as interpretations
of Asian conventions. She embroiders on Asian models rather than
attempting to emulate them. For example, in *Twelfth Night* and *Sihanouk*
she uses spectacular, oversized silk parasols, prompted by kabuki but
danced across the stage in a mincing step reminiscent of Indian dance.
For *Richard II*, she imagines costumes that combine elements of samurai
warrior kimonos with Elizabethan doublets and ruffs from an earlier
period. She invents new forms based on forms she has studied, for
instance the speaking actor/puppets with their actor/puppeteers of
Drums on the Dam, inspired by bunraku theater. Critic Adrian Kiernander
praises Mnouchkine's turn to Asia as a real breakthrough in advancing
Western performance practice:

> [Mnouchkine opens up] the relationship between the elements of
> stage signs, to make the processes of devising and reading a production
> part of a more interesting and flexible act than straightforward mechanical
> substitution.
>
> (Kiernander 1992: 153)

He lauds her work for doing precisely what she intends: challenging her
spectators by surprising them, by insisting that they rid themselves of
the clichés that come too easily in performance in order to plumb the
inner space of the theater piece at hand.

Mnouchkine's penchant for, and appreciation of, Asian theater stems
in great part from its status as total theater, a theater that fuses music,
dance, art, and the sacred. She is summoned by this completeness to
develop a total vision of her own, one in which what she calls the "working rules [of] gestural precision, clarity of line, [. . .] extreme truth and
extreme artifice" come together in performance – a movement-theater
that has the feel of a concentrated and balanced ritual (program notes,
Richard II 1980). The apogee of this effort was no doubt *The House of
Atreus Cycle* in which the four highly choreographed and very different
choruses captured through costume, movement, cries, and shouts, as
well as through the empathic tension of their listening bodies onstage,
the emotional tenor of the whole cycle – and of each separate

play: female sacrifice (*Iphigenia*), patriarchal ruthlessness and civic impotency (*Agamemnon*), the somber criminality of Orestes (*The Libation Bearers*), and the potential for the hidden revenge of matriarchy crushed by law (*The Eumenides*).

When Mnouchkine speaks of Asian theater, we hear clear parallels with her thoughts about working with masks. For her, Asian theater is the site of living signs in motion. It offers a phenomenal but controlled physicality that permits immediate and tactile contact with the public:

> What interests me in Asian tradition is the place of the actor as a creator of metaphors. The actor's art consists in showing passion, in recounting a human being's insides. Through Asian theatre, I realized that the actor's mission was to open up the human being like a pomegranate – not in order to show human guts, but in order to sketch them, display them in signs, in forms, in movement, in rhythm.
>
> (Féral 2001: 17–18)

In Asian-inspired theater, the actor is king, the conduit between the public and the force field of the theatrical piece, a vector to a different world, one of aesthetic pleasure and of spirituality. Whether through mask work or other Asian- influenced theatrical techniques (Figure 2.2), the actor for Mnouchkine, like the puppet evoked by Kleist in 1812, becomes the point of congruence for connecting mind and matter, soul and body, "true theater" and theater-making.

THE ROLE OF THE ACTOR

As we have highlighted, in Ariane Mnouchkine's affirmations, as well as in her practice, the actor holds the pride of place. From the point of contact for a historical lesson to conduit to the concentrated energy of life, Mnouchkine's ideal actor focuses the public's desire. Of late, Mnouchkine's more sustained commentaries have revealed more clearly her own role as teacher and trainer of actors. The actor's role, as part of a collective, has very obviously evolved.

In the early years of the company (1964–72), the "actors," mostly students of the humanities – including Mnouchkine – were learning together to be actors, to make theater, and to invent a new institution that embodied their socialist ideals. All were looking for a style of acting that would best permit them to tell a story. And the lessons purloined

Figure 2.2 The actor Juliana Carneiro da Cunha, masked as a *bunraku* puppet, as Lord Khang in *Drums on the Dam*, 1999

from Jacques Lecoq (1966–7) and learned during a foundational summer sojourn (1968) at an abandoned salt works in Arc-en-Senans made it possible for them, in a first phase, to improvise with masks. This, in turn, helped them generate texts on themes proposed principally by Mnouchkine.

By 1979 many of these early comrades (with more to follow) had left the collective to form their own companies, to work freelance, or solo. The effort of the new members was thereafter concentrated more on collectively improvising the form and shape of scenes than on collectively devising texts. Mnouchkine, with her accumulated experience and years, and her renewed encounters with non-Western theater, became even more patently the leader, the pedagogue, and the architect. She also became more willing to speak out on what an actor must be.

To be an actor with the Soleil, Mnouchkine implies, one must have high energy, imaginative depth, physical strength and daring, and a hunger to achieve and give:

> You need strong calves. [...] And by that I mean the freest possible body but also the best trained. But you also need strong calves of the imagination – and by that I mean the freest and best-trained imagination possible.
>
> (Féral 2001: 52)

Mnouchkine believes in talent and takes on board only those who have it. She is particularly drawn to those actors who demonstrate intense curiosity, who have a boundless ability to play.

For Mnouchkine, theater work begins with the search for characters. This is the actors' fundamental contribution to a production and, as we have seen, is initiated by working with masks. The process may begin with actors losing their moorings and, consequently, their sense of who they are. But once actors give up their anchor, they move into a space of calmness, of creativity and openness to the themes and emotional states Mnouchkine proposes. Improvisations evolve from this search and develop into scenes. Actors, Mnouchkine says, should not concentrate on putting across the text, exploring an idea, or understanding the role. To find the character, they must banish individual psychology. There should be no sub-text and no playing the un-said.

At the same time, actors must connect to the emotion the character experiences. This can lead to the same difficulties actors encounter in a more method-oriented process. For example, Maurice Durozier, with the Soleil since 1981, had to drop out of the *House of Atreus* production because, as a new father, he absolutely resisted finding the emotion that would lead him, as Agamemnon does in the play, to sacrifice his child. There was, then, no question of his working to transform this emotion into a physical sign.

Mnouchkine defines an actor as "a person who metaphorizes a feeling" (Williams 1999: 96). Actors must find this feeling – characterized by Mnouchkine as a "state" (or an internal landscape or essential chord) – and isolate it physically. In performance, each state must be followed by the next state, with some kind of marker between them. Mnouchkine counsels: "One can only show successive states, in ruptured discontinuity" (Williams 1999: 96). Through the tension created in isolating states, the characters will often appear to be subjected to a double constraint – as if pulled on high and anchored from below, like a puppet whose strings are being expertly pulled.

Mnouchkine insists on the collective building of characters. She does not cast her productions at the beginning of rehearsals. This forces the actors to be on, to be present, at every moment. In principle, this can mean that each character contains all of the others, as many different actors will try out many of the same roles. What is sure is that this process layers each character, actors building on the improvisations that have already worked. Some actors assume the role of master actor, or locomotive, a technique that Mnouchkine has utilized to great effect since the late 1980s. During improvisations, master actors are shadowed by imitators who absorb what the master actors suggest. The imitator may or may not end up in the role, but will have contributed to building it.

This type of collective work in building characters has had spectacular results in creating the choruses that have become salient aspects of Mnouchkine's productions since, especially, *The House of Atreus Cycle*. It made possible the work on *Drums on the Dam*, in which the actor/puppets and actor/puppeteers manipulating them had to identify totally with one another. Such mind and body twinning can also, however, disturb the actor who does not win the role he or she has been rehearsing. The documentary film on Mnouchkine's rehearsals for *Tartuffe, Au Soleil même la nuit* (1997), shows us just how painful this was in the attempt to find the character Damis. Myriam Azencot, a longtime actor with the Soleil, remarks on the struggle twinning initiates for both seasoned and junior members of the collective: "[In the collective building of characters] you have to let go of a lot of things. You have to let go of your control and you really have to let go of your ego" (Féral 1998: 139). The creativity of the group, however, can also fuel the individual's ability to move forward, to find the shape of an emotion or an idea.

THE ROLE OF THE PUBLIC

Theater happens, according to Mnouchkine, in the meeting between public and performers. Without a public, theater cannot be. Thus she has spent much time and energy imagining and trying to realize what her public should be. She has often commented on her ideal public, remarks that unsurprisingly recall those designating her ideal actor. The public must be made conscious of its own potential for playfulness, for innocence, and for belief: "I want the spectators to listen to the child within themselves, to have the courage to resist the disenchantment, the irony, and the absence of hope all around us" (Féral 1998: 38). Spectators must, however, also work to determine what the play is saying:

> [S]pectators must be left with things to discover. These are waves, resonances; an actor strikes a gong or drops a pebble in water, but he won't try to fix all of the waves that will be emitted, to freeze them so that everyone can clearly count the number of rings that are released.
>
> (Williams 1999: 84)

Mnouchkine's ideal public must, then, actively participate in the work of reception and interpretation; but it should also allow itself to be carried away and freed, to receive as a child, without preconceptions.

As discussed earlier, Mnouchkine has imagined innovative ways of including her public in the elaboration of her productions – from consultation and physical participation in the early years to sensory immersion and complex identification in later productions. Moreover, she has established an organization for contacting and maintaining a community of spectators who stay as committed to the work of the Soleil as do members of the company. Like the theaters in France's public sector, the Soleil has settled on a pricing system and a networking that permit non-wealthy people, and especially students of modest means (about 100 students per night), to go to the theater. She cultivates a following that accompanies the work from the early festive evenings at which she presents the project to its realization in performance. In 2004, the high school *baccalaureat* exam for specialists in theater arts centered on the work of the Théâtre du Soleil, thereby cementing the crucial place of the Soleil in the imaginary of France's secondary students. The Théâtre du Soleil is, in other words, the theater with which one grows up.

Perhaps the most stunning positioning of the public as integral to the Soleil's work rests in the architecture of the theater. The Cartoucherie's three vast halls with their womb-like warmth englobe the public in a joyful pilgrimage. Moving into and through these grotto-like spaces takes on, and is meant to take on, the force of a transporting ritual. Like all proper rituals, this one is organized in steps. As there are no assigned seats, spectators arrive at least an hour before the play begins and enter the theater to claim a place. Mnouchkine, herself, opens the double doors to the first hall after gathering the actors together and pronouncing the ritual phrase: "The public enters!" (Féral 2001: 96). This catches the actors up, reminding them of their own commitment, while, at the same time, theatricalizing the work of the public.

Spectators enjoy whatever is displayed in the first hall (sometimes grandiose maps, books related to the theater project, publications by the Soleil). They may eat together at this point, or at intermission. The proffered and always enticingly perfumed meal, will be prepared and served by both production crew and actors and will connect to the performance by referencing the culture that has inspired the theater piece. Actors and audience thus partake in a communion that nourishes both body and soul. In the second hall, spectators may also watch actors prepare for performance. The dressing rooms, built under the bleachers, strategically open up to viewing, so that audience members can catch a glimpse of actors finishing their make up, dressing, or meditating. This will be the public's first contact with the always exquisite costumes, elaborate make-up or masks, and strong colors – most often reds and ochres – of the production. This visual encounter also forms part of the public's initiation.

These ritual steps, the extreme congeniality of the welcome – with Mnouchkine herself greeting the spectators streaming in from the park where the theater is located – the length of each production (an average of 4 hours), the sensuality of the experience – all contrive to immerse the spectators in the world of the production. In witnessing this process over the years, Mnouchkine has located her spectators' longing for the sacred, a nostalgic reaction in these secular times which leaves them looking, according to her, like "gilled humans" (Williams 1999: 90).

Her intention, however, is not to have them regress to some atavistic state but, rather, to permit them to dwell comfortably, at least for the duration of the experience, in a space of wonder. During the run of *The House of Atreus Cycle*, for example, to reach their seats spectators had to walk over a huge excavated chasm in which life-sized terra cotta figures, replicas of the choral members in *Agamemnon*, marched in serried rows. When the chorus of actors entered the playing space, it was as if the dream figures haunting the excavation site had come to life.

THE CREATIVE PROCESS

MNOUCHKINE'S ROLE AS DIRECTOR

While one might think of Ariane Mnouchkine as the axis around which the Soleil rotates, the company's pivot and direction-giver, she also characterizes herself – at least during the rehearsal period – as being in symbiosis with actors, designers, and other collaborators. She feels dependent on and pregnable to their ideas. She does not know at the outset of the rehearsal period exactly what she wants to achieve. She does not even know how long the rehearsal process will be. (A Soleil production averages six months of rehearsal time.)

She does begin each new project with a concept or theme, one that might initiate a new text by Cixous or a collective script by the company or one that underlies the selection of a specific theater text. She also has a host of images to share with actors and designers. Her process is, in fact, overwhelmingly visual. Thus, from the moment rehearsals begin, she determines (in collaboration with the costumers) the costume aesthetic. This will almost always be based in bold primary colors, especially red, yellow, black, and white, as in *The House of Atreus Cycle*. She will use color as part of the signifying process. For example, the female chorus of Euripide's *Iphigenia* was figured in white with red sashes and protuberant tummy pads. This conveyed at once the importance of the theme of maternity, the purity of Iphigenia herself, and the bloodiness to come in Agamemnon's sacrifice of his child. The costumes reinforced Mnouchkine's reading of *The House of Atreus* as a series of crimes based in militaristic and patriarchal misogyny.

Mnouchkine also primes rehearsals with photographs, illustrations, and metaphors. To give form, for example, in *Tartuffe*, to the ferocious and desperate strength of Dorine confronting her angry and bewitched master Orgon, Mnouchkine showed the actors a drawing of an enraged monkey fending off a charging tiger (see *Au Soleil même la nuit*, the documentary on rehearsing *Tartuffe*). This provoked a series of improvisations that led to the energetic antagonism linking these two characters.

The typical, almost iconic photograph of Mnouchkine during rehearsals portrays her watching intently, with all her body alert, surrounded by actors also watching intently as another group of actors improvises (Figure 2.3). In rehearsals, she comments, prods, suggests – and the actors move with these suggestions, unless they get stuck. Mnouchkine will occasionally get stuck with them. Sometimes an actor finds the way out. Eventually, the cascading improvisations lead to a moment when Mnouchkine sees what she wants. This seeing encompasses the actors and other collaborators, who, if the process is working, catch the rightness of the moment with her: All understand organically the direction of the performance as it is taking place. Sophie Moscoso, Mnouchkine's assistant on every production until *Le Dernier Caravansérail*, describes how this process of collective seeing works:

> When a minute of theatre finally happens, and I mean by that a minute of truth, of life in a form, everybody sees it; the bleachers [from where all are watching] tremble. And then Ariane articulates what has happened. [. . .] She guides us, taking us even farther.
>
> (Féral 1998: 108)

Mnouchkine does all the cleaning up, removing "the barnacles," as actor Juliana Carneiro da Cunha puts it (Féral 1998: 30), before fixing once and for all the scenes and transitions. Meticulous and perfectionist, she also always builds in off nights during a production's run (usually twelve months) to recalibrate the performance. After years of relying on her assistant's memory, Mnouchkine now has her rehearsals videotaped. These she reviews in the evening, deciding what to keep and show of the improvisations at the next day's rehearsals. The performance builds on these selections.

THE REHEARSAL

The Théâtre du Soleil spends no time analyzing the text or the project's idea at the first rehearsal. There is no work around the table, no

Figure 2.3
Ariane
Mnouchkine
(seated on
bleachers),
Hélène Cixous
(at desk), and
the company
during a
rehearsal of
l'Indiade, 1987

dramaturgical lectures – as there are in so many Brechtian-inspired French companies, whose directors are of Mnouchkine's generation. From the beginning, Mnouchkine and the actors are in a mode of discovery and creation, rather than interpretation or repetition. The set is not built, other than the empty 14 × 14 square meter platform on which the actors rehearse; and scenes are not worked in any special order. Mnouchkine tells the story of what they will attempt to create. This initial narrative is the crucial moment for establishing the tone, the outlook and the goal of the production. Actors might be encouraged to do their own research (such as reading up on AIDS for *The Perjured City*) or they might even travel beforehand (a joint voyage to India for *l'Indiade*). But their time on the rehearsal stage will be spent in improvising, after donning costumes and masks or make-up that will help establish the characters. (Rehearsal costumes are culled and rearranged from the impressive stock of old costumes stored at the Cartoucherie.) Very often the shapes and textures put together by the actors will inspire what the costumers build.

There will usually be two or three months of rehearsals before a consensus is reached that the feel is right. Then the designers go ahead and execute the performance costumes, the set pieces, and the final music. Casting is also done at this point. Those actors who are not cast will spend their time in the workshops, kitchen, or administration, or on the technical aspects of the show, including physically carrying out the set changes.

THE ROLE OF KEY COLLABORATORS

As central as is the role of actors to Mnouchkine's process, three key collaborators form with her the imaginary carpet on which the actors travel and create. These three artists – Jean-Jacques Lemêtre, Guy-Claude François, and Erhard Stiefel – constitute the design core of the Soleil. They have complemented and furthered Mnouchkine's search for a transcendent theatrical experience since the 1970s. Her accomplishments as a director and the particular texture of her productions would be unthinkable without the collaboration of these men.

Jean-Jacques Lemêtre: the sound and the fury

Of the three, Jean-Jacques Lemêtre, with the Soleil since 1979, is most involved in the day to day rehearsal process. Musician, instrument maker, composer, and teacher, Lemêtre improvises alongside the actors, often (as in the case of *The Shakespeare Cycle*) finding or making an instrument to match the emotional timber of the actor's state. At first, he will follow actors with a drum, helping to fix the pace and the rhythm by keeping the actor performing as though dancing. Lemêtre chooses his instruments according to the images evoked. He may, as for *Henri IV, Part I*, end up with as many as 300 instruments onstage, located on the side platform built to house him and his assistants.

He helps clarify the move from emotional state to emotional stage by changing instruments, using primarily winds and percussions made of metal or wood. Lemêtre has also helped develop the vocal characteristics peculiar to Soleil actors: a voice pitched from the chest and the head and emanating from the higher vocal registers. This voice is close to a singer's and thus better dovetails with the musical accompaniment.

Lemêtre's work reinforces the iconic nature and precise metaphorization of each characterization. His participation has been determinate, for example, in creating the exhilarating high-energy entrances and exits for which the Soleil is known. His music, never neutral, draws in the public with its seductive and expressive quality. The oddly chant-like voice he has encouraged has also helped create the ritual feel of the productions. Lemêtre has learned how to accompany the text without drowning it, how to be part of the movement of the text by punctuating it. He fixes his scoring in a quasi-magical collusion with Mnouchkine, with whom he has developed a sixth sense for knowing when the sound and images are right.

Guy-Claude François: the space of wonder

Guy-Claude François, like Lemêtre, an innovative, multitalented theater person, has worked side by side with Mnouchkine since 1968. Together, they continue to explore the possibilities of affecting a new dynamic between actors and audience through spatial configurations. François has developed out of the "noble" materials of marble and stone the permanent, unframed frontal space that Mnouchkine has proclaimed – since the early 1980s – best for epic storytelling. The fantastic, bulky costumes and extraordinary masks or make-up worn by her actors communicate meaning most efficaciously in a face to face confrontation with the audience. With this frontal space, François and Mnouchkine approach what they believe to be a modern ideal in staging dimensions: a 14 × 14 square meter central playing area replicated by the space allotted to the keenly raked bleachers where the audience sits.

François adjusts this vast empty space according to the requirements of each production. He creates partitions, walls, half-walls, ramps (*The House of Atreus Cycle*); fences and enclosures (*Tartuffe*); niches (*The Perjured City*); steps down to the audience (*l'Indiade*) as the need for them presents itself to Mnouchkine and the actors during improvisations. Of late, the monumental and meditative space of such productions as *The Perjured City* has taken on the contours (through draping and lighting) of a more delicate and intimate floating dream space. This unanchored and transformable space is "named" through the positioning of separate but highly charged markers – such as the trees, bushes, and wagons of *Le Dernier Caravansérail*.

Much of what happens in a Mnouchkine production happens outside what would be a traditional box frame. Characters emerge and disappear from traps under the playing area or under the seated audience. François' architectural spaces thus must accommodate a complex lighting plan to capture these moments of transition. First, however, the lights must be able to catch the eyes and the angles of masks for the frontal displays. They must also be able to sweep the sides, runways, and vomitorium running under the fixed bleachers. His spaces always, also, absorb and reflect the soft glow from the ceiling grid, itself often draped in translucent cloth. This multiplaned space and the lighting that extends into and encompasses the public help create a fusion of spaces superimposed one on the other, as in the work of imagination and reverie.

Erhard Stiefel: the "soul" of acting

Mnouchkine has always known how to find and nurture exceptional talents, people whose sensibilities and energies both complement and stimulate her own aesthetic sense. The company sculptor, Erhard Stiefel, has been in her orbit since 1967, setting up his own mask-making studio on her invitation in a corner of the Soleil's space in the Cartoucherie. Stiefel has ballasted and rendered concrete her commitment to the art and necessity of working with masks.

Like Mnouchkine, Stiefel was a student of Jacques Lecoq in the 1960s. He discovered the power of masks first while apprenticing in Milan with Amleto Sartori, who, with Lecoq revived *commedia dell'arte* style for **Giorgio Strehler**'s Piccolo theater. Under Sartori's and

Lecoq's guidance, Stiefel came to see masks – but not just any mask, only successfully wrought ones – as having their own life force. For Stiefel, great masks are holy: They must be honored as such and treasured for what they teach us about channeling energy and experiencing a totally different body from our own. Stiefel has made over forty masks for the Soleil, from both the *commedia dell'arte* and Topeng traditions. He has also built articulated body masks (the bear from *l'Indiade*, the donkey from *Le Dernier Caravansérail*); both monumental and diminutive puppet witnesses (the life-sized terra cotta statuary for *The House of Atreus*, the 700 witnessing dolls representing massacred Cambodians for *Sihanouk*); Japanese-inspired cloth masks (all the actor/puppets for *Drums on the Dam*); and myriad sizes and shapes of false noses (for a third of the characters in *Le Dernier Caravansérail*). His very presence in the heart of the company makes a statement about what constitutes the soul of acting for Mnouchkine. She can count on him to help visualize all possible forms that mask work might take.

THE ROLE OF THE THEATRICAL TEXT

With Stiefel watching over their "soul," François their "space," and Lemêtre their "rhythm," it often falls to the internationally known thinker and writer Hélène Cixous to watch over the words of the Théâtre du Soleil. Since her early-1980s encounter with the Soleil, Cixous has been involved in some way in every project. She has, most notably, produced four full texts (*l'Indiade*, *Sihanouk*, *The Perjured City*, and *Drums on the Dam*), each based on a Mnouchkine idea. Yet Mnouchkine still exerts considerable influence in the writing sphere, uneasy, as she always has been, about the role of the text in the collective process. We might even suggest that she feels as free to jettison and alter texts as she does to tamper with music, space, and masks.

Mnouchkine had been circling around the idea of a company writer practically from the beginning of her career. In the early years, running up against the limits of improvisation, she frequently expressed frustration at not having someone who could write the great French historical epic for modern times. But she has also vacillated continuously in her attitude toward texts. She has categorically refused the kind of text-based theater that privileges diction and evacuates telling with the body. To avoid such a pitfall, she has even tried her own hand at adaptation (*Méphisto*) and translation (*The Shakespeare Cycle*; and *Agamemnon* and

The Libation Bearers of *The House of Atreus Cycle*). By her own admission, translating has meant specifically working on the target text's rhythmic potential, clarity of images, and energy fields. In this, we can see that she is thinking like a director more interested in big emotions and grand gestures than in what a text might present in nuances, shadings, gray zones, and ambiguities. (Accordingly, her production of *Twelfth Night*, which raucously exteriorized the delicate internal conflict of Orsino, was less well received than her choreography of power struggles in *Richard II*.)

When Mnouchkine speaks of texts, including the epic texts she admires – the Greeks, Shakespeare, Cixous – she posits a curious variation on the conundrum of the chicken and the egg. It is as if the actor (i.e. her masked actor), might well come before the verse – the writer being displaced all together:

> If the body of the actor is possessed by the body of the character, by what we might call the mask, then, at that moment, the text becomes its secretions, its drool, its peepee, its poop, its breath, its saliva, its blood.
>
> (Féral 1998: 34)

The mask would seem to produce the text, rather than being informed by it. Indeed, even when Mnouchkine works with fully scripted texts, the actors improvise by approximating lines, only learning the printed text at the last minute. In her most recent collective works (*Et Soudain des nuits d'éveil* and *Le Dernier Caravansérail*), the texts produced through this constant invention sometimes lack a satisfying dramatic structure. They tend to wander, despite the crispness of the images and the energy of the music.

Even when working with Cixous, Mnouchkine is so concerned by a process that keeps everyone in the present that she will often start rehearsals well before Cixous has finished the last scene. This does preclude actors playing to an ending. It also keeps them awake to discovery. But this also keeps Cixous at the drawing board, rewriting, and being "rewritten" sometimes up to the last weeks of rehearsals. (The original text for *Drums on the Dam*, for example, was over 400 pages long. The final running time of the show was $3\frac{1}{2}$ hours based on a seventy-six page text that had been extensively chopped and reframed during rehearsals.)

Hélène Cixous' contribution

Despite the Soleil's editing of her texts, or perhaps because she has wholeheartedly eased herself into the collaborative mentality, Cixous has been an exceptional partner to Mnouchkine. She has both shaped and helped forge Mnouchkine's most recent articulation of theater as a transformative space. In her writings on theater, she has named this space, "the space of the invited other," where even she, as writer, becomes possessed by the characters called forth (*l'Indiade*: 256). A border-crosser in genre, Cixous also crosses borders in her Shakespearian-inspired theater texts: between the living and the dead, between the comic and the tragic, between dreams and awakenings, between eras, between houses. She has the pen necessary to grasp Mnouchkine's imaginative scope, while Mnouchkine has the sparky ideas and directorial authority to stoke and discipline Cixous' lyrical unreservedness.

Cixous has also theorized the work of the Soleil in her postface to *l'Indiade* in terms that convincingly include Mnouchkine in a feminist project. She attributes to Mnouchkine's *mises-en-scène* the generous and multifaceted energy, the nonhierarchical but overflowing movement, the all-embracing sensuality that characterize her own notion of "feminine writing." Moreover, Cixous' influence has helped Mnouchkine create major roles for women actors, mostly decentered in productions up to *The Perjured City*. While Mnouchkine has never objectified her female characters, while there has never been any cheap sexuality in her productions, in her attempts to capture history with its concentration on "great men," she has sometimes missed the women warriors toiling in history's background. In recent collaborations, notably *The Perjured City* and *Drums on the Dam*, the central characters have, on the contrary, been deeply charismatic women.

PARADOXES AND TENSIONS

It is not hyperbolic to say that Ariane Mnouchkine is the most powerful woman in French theater and one of the world's greatest living directors. Her ability to invent new theatrical forms, to dazzle the imagination and the senses with every production, her unfailing commitment to political action in life and through theater, her courage to speak out against prevailing mentalities and received ideas — including about how theater should work — set her apart from those in her generation who have lost faith, or lost themselves, in the French theatrical system. Nevertheless, her insistence on collaborative theater, on exploring a theatricalized other, and on pushing to the limits experimentations with Asian techniques have led to certain recurring tensions and even potential contradictions. These tensions have affected the functioning of the company and have prompted a number of critics to question the soundness of her process and the political correctness of her vision.

INDIVIDUAL ASPIRATIONS AND THE COLLECTIVE

Much has been made of the noisy departures of key performers of the Théâtre du Soleil. In his clever and nervous one-man shows *Ariane ou l'Age d'Or* [Ariane or The Age of Gold] and *Jours de Colère: Ariane II* [Days of Wrath: Ariane II], Philippe Caubère (Abdallah in *l'Age d'Or*, Molière in the film of the same name) has, as mentioned earlier, even made a solid career of theatrically reprimanding Mnouchkine's ardent directorial style. Every several years, actors who have functioned as master actors or locomotives (Caubère, Philippe Hottier, Georges Bigot, Simon Abkarian, Catherine Schaub, to name a few) leave the company. Some, like Caubère and Hottier, angrily slam the door of the Cartoucherie and protest "Ariane's" excessive control. For Mnouchkine, these departures never stop hurting. It is like a wound in her "maternal body" (Williams 1999: 124).

There is no question that to be an actor with the Soleil, one has to submit to a grueling work schedule (at times from 9:00 in the morning until 12:00 at night), a schedule that includes manual labor and the possibility of not performing. Actors must give themselves up totally to the life of the company. The older actors cannot always keep up the pace, while the youngest actors tend to stay, mesmerized by the unparalleled quality of the work and by the fact of being part of a company that is now mythic. Others, many of whose creative strengths have been fundamental to certain productions (Bigot and Hottier in the Shakespeares, Abkarian and Schaub in *The House of Atreus Cycle*) have had to spread their wings and finally make their own artistic decisions. Some, used to a style of performance and a mode of functioning unlike anything else in France's theater world, are unable to adapt to theatrical life outside the Soleil. Often their training with Mnouchkine proves to be nontransferable to other theater venues or to television and film work.

One way to understand the turmoil between Mnouchkine and some of her actors is that she has been living her own utopian dream since 1964. It would seem that either one enters this dream or leaves it. What is now unquestionable is that she is the person who holds the dream together: The collective grows out of her will and is reinforced by the continuing presence of her closest collaborators. She thus feels that she must run a tough and tight ship. We might go back to the several images we have proposed that suggest that Mnouchkine directs her actors as if they were marionettes. This can have the aesthetic result of creating a coherent, hieratic, choreographed performance in which bodies tell as much of the tale as the text. However, if the actors are not fully invested in the process, or if they have had their own ideas clipped in order to conform to Mnouchkine's vision, then puppetry might connote psychologically the actors' feeling of impotency. In any case, if an actor cannot accept that Mnouchkine's is the final word in the collective process, then he or she must take leave.

In our highly individualistic times, the possibility of such a collective functioning at all is truly remarkable. Hence, we can appreciate the intelligence behind Mnouchkine's refocusing on collective creation of characters and scenes rather than on texts. That she has returned to collective writing in 2003 for *Le Dernier Caravansérail*, nonetheless, shows that she has not yet renounced believing in the possibility of a collective "mind." Nor does she lack the will power and the sense of discovery to recommit to theater every time one group of actors leaves and a new group forms. (The some forty-member acting company renews itself by a third or a half at the outset of almost every production, new actors coming on board recruited from her workshops.) Every time she reveals to a new group how mask work can transform theater, she feels she is planting the seeds for the future. We might, then, think of the collective itself as a continuously spiraling group of humans (now some 500 people strong), with some spiraling off and others being pulled in, but with all being permanently altered by the magnetism of the experience.

THE ORIENTALIST CRITIQUE

Of the criticisms levied against Ariane Mnouchkine, the most ferocious and muddled has targeted what some have felt to be her appropriation of forms and stories that do not belong to Western culture. This has been part of a more generalized debate on interculturalism in the theater and whether or not cultural borrowings and hybridization are a healthy theatrical development or yet another way for more economically powerful Western cultures to colonize less economically secure ones. Within this debate, Mnouchkine has been chastised for treating from too great a distance and without deep understanding historical moments of great import to "developing world" cultures; that is, cultures that have been subjected to the greater power and influence of Europe and North America (Anne-Marie Picard 1989). She has been blamed for misrepresenting venerable Eastern theatrical traditions that she has not been immersed in since childhood (Issacharoff and Jones 1988). Her productions of the Shakespearian plays and *l'Indiade*, in particular – grouped together with a criticism of Peter Brook's 9-hour theatrical recreation of the Indian sacred epic, *The Mahabharata* – have been negatively characterized as "sterile imitation" at worst (Pavis 1996: 81) and "naïve" (Pavis 1992: 198) at best. The ruckus has finally subsided and a form of consensus seems to have been reached that some forms of cultural borrowing can be part of the process of cultural understanding. Moreover, no one really wants to stand by a proclamation that would seem to deny artists their right to freedom of expression or experimentation with form.

Nevertheless, it is legitimate to worry about the nature of the reception of these works. Denis Salter notes what he calls the "intentional paradox" of Mnouchkine's characters in *l'Indiade*: they seem "real" but are also transposed by stage conventions into something not quite real (Salter 1993). It could very well be that these conventions are less obvious to spectators used to realism; and thus that such a public sees a direct transposition of Indian culture – in what would be a kind of **orientalist** minstrel show.

Minstrelry (making oneself up as "the other" to take the other over, to evacuate difference, to control representation) is indeed a dangerous and unethical practice. If Mnouchkine's spectators do not perceive the heightened realism, the effect of strange-making in *Sihanouk*, *l'Indiade*, or, more recently, *Le Dernier Caravansérail*, they might, in fact, see a production that speaks to "the truth of Asia," rather than a production that uses Asia as a fiction or metaphor to speak about civil war, trauma, and displacement as conditions of modernity. Therein lies a potential tension between what Mnouchkine means to achieve and how she might be understood. The quality of the acting is central to deflating this tension. The more tightly choreographed, the better the concentration, the more precise the movements, the more the spectators will see the work as "representation" rather than reality.

We would submit that there is a certain positive naivety in Mnouchkine's humanistic vision, in her desire to decrease the space between the **Western self** as referent and the other she puts onstage. Naivety is germane to her utopian effort to unite the human community. And while naive efforts have led to egregious acts of colonialism in the past (as in the case of certain Christian missions), we also know that, deployed with sensitivity and intelligence, efforts at uniting are the only kinds of efforts that attempt to build an internationalism not based on economic control. We would also add that theater companies from Asia and Africa are also participating in intercultural theater – not as a means of avenging their colonization by the West, but as a way of expanding their own representational repertory. Finally, it could be, as critic Marvin Carlson concludes, that the question is less about interculturalism than transculturalism – or, again, a way of striving to find theatrical and human truths that cut across nations, cultures, and time frames (Pavis 1996: 88).

THE FORMALIST ACCUSATION

Related to the debate over cultural appropriation is the objection to the extreme formalism of Mnouchkine's productions. Both charges are intimately connected to her integration, reinterpretation, and invention of Asian or Asian-like theater forms, be they variants of Korean drumming, Japanese bunraku, Noh or kabuki, Indian dance, or even Armenian folk dance. Critics gently lament the early phase of Mnouchkine's work, in which the obvious gestures of theater pointing to itself as theater and of actors self-consciously stepping outside of characters heightened and oriented the political commentary (Bradby and Delgado 2002). One can, of course, worry about the so-called un-thinking catharsis that comes with being so swept away by the beauty, panorama, scale, virtuosity, and melodrama of a Mnouchkine production that any moral or political lesson is lost. However, it would be wiser to take a more sophisticated approach to identification and the question of aesthetic pleasure. Neither identification nor distanciation are simple, one-step processes.

For Anthony Tatlow, who examines a healthy selection of world-wide productions of Shakespeare in his book *Shakespeare, Brecht, and The Intercultural Sign*, Mnouchkine's excessive formalism does exactly what she means it to do – makes us aware in a process that both distances and pulls us in of what passes for "normal":

> Mnouchkine appears to essentialize, to concentrate on an extreme externalization of the emotional life that no longer locates and explains it in relation to historical experience. But when the emotional states are so compellingly reimagined and when such performance shatters our percep-tual habits, we have the opportunity of reperceiving. [...] What Mnouchkine does is an extension of what Brecht imagined, partly realized, but largely left undone: the development of an aesthetically compelling style, that gracefulness, which enables us to perceive a truth obscured by habituation.
>
> (Tatlow 2001: 62)

Tatlow believes that Mnouchkine's "compelling style" allows us to apprehend historical operations at work. In other words, through formal experimentation, Mnouchkine brings us to a place of enlighten-ment, if not action. Again, it would seem that reception is everything; and that to be enlightened the public must wish to see. Mnouchkine, indeed, does her best to prime her audience. Through explanatory programs and also pre-performance information and preparation in the Cartoucherie itself, she attempts to attract and form spectators apt to reflect on the link between their own social engagement and the meaning of her productions.

Mnouchkine: the good magus

Victoria Nelson, in her book *The Secret Life of Puppets*, reminds us of "how utterly unsophisticated the tenets of eighteenth-century rational-ism have left us, believers and unbelievers alike, in that complex area we blithely dub *spiritual*" (Nelson 2001: 288). Nelson thinks that we are in the midst of an epistemological shift in which the spiritual (or that which is outside the realm of reason and logic) is regaining credibility, not as something grotesque or uneasy, but as a separate and essential domain of knowing. If this is so, Mnouchkine is squarely within this movement. Her search for the transcendent through theatrical form combines several ways of knowing and implicates several domains of human experience, including the historical and the political. For Mnouchkine, the body's truth is as real as any mental imaging, and her corporeally focused actors are both purveyors of immortality and conduits to other forms of consciousness. By not freezing her art through endless reproduction of the same form, Mnouchkine does not fall into sterile aesthetization. She neither neutralizes the spiritual nor evacuates the historical. A good magus, she creates through beauty a theater world that accesses a feeling of sacredness; but she also sheds light on necessary, if difficult, choices.

3

FOUR KEY PRODUCTIONS

Mnouchkine's "Fanatically Theatrical"

I'm not someone who believes in a *tabula rasa*. It's true we've spent a lot of time looking for our sources, sources that make us rich. Nothing is invented, nothing is created, everything is transformed. That goes for art as well. There's what we might call a great ancestral river which thousands of actors navigate, inventing the theatre each time. I always want to swim in the currents of that stream.

(Lecoq 1987: 128)

Ariane Mnouchkine's theater work can be examined as an ongoing effort to experiment with and synthesize traditional theatrical forms in order to create something entirely new – and often totally astonishing. As she has frequently indicated, and as we have seen, she likes to dive into the diverse currents that have defined theater, especially European popular forms and Asian traditions, in order to reinterpret and recombine them, shaking up and in the process viscerally connecting actors, audience, and critics. This chapter explores the movement and the continuity in her innovative theater work by in-depth analyses of four productions: the Théâtre du Soleil's collective creation – *1789 or The Revolution Must Only Stop at the Perfection of Happiness* (1971–2); Shakespeare's *Richard II* (1981); Hélène Cixous' *l'Indiade* (1987); and finally Cixous' *Drums on the Dam – In the Form of an Ancient Puppet Play Performed by Actors* (1999). Each of these productions, which altogether cover some thirty years of

Mnouchkine's career, has been hailed as a theatrical milestone, resulting in Mnouchkine's workshops being the most sought after of any in Europe by young actors from all over the world (Bradby and Delgaldo 2002: 130). Each, also, speaks cogently to more generalized tendencies in contemporary theater and theatrical development.

1789: COLLECTIVE CREATION, AUDIENCE INVOLVEMENT, AND COMEDIC FORM

Of the Théâtre du Soleil's twenty-six theatrical productions since its founding in 1964, *1789* remains the most celebrated, achieving legendary status as the kind of production that marks theater history, signaling a major change in how the doing of theatre can be both thought and accomplished. Critic and teacher Bernard Dort in 1973 already understood how the production and its sequel *1793 or La Cité Révolutionnaire est de ce monde* (1973) had galvanized French theater when he commented: "For almost three years now, the center of gravity of French theater has been called *1789–1793*" (Dort 1973: 9). Some 250,000 spectators (a record number for French productions) participated in the theatrical experience that was *1789* (which also traveled to Italy, the United Kingdom, Germany, Yugoslavia, Switzerland, and Martinique). Thousands more have seen the Mnouchkine directed film of the production (1974) that successfully captures the feel of a high energy, kaleidoscopic, visual, and emotional romp through the events of the first year of the French Revolution. Of all the ways that we might examine this piece to establish its centrality in the development of theater work in the last half of the twentieth century, the most fruitful assess three related aspects: (1) the ways in which Mnouchkine and the company pursued a collective approach to creating the work, (2) the inventions which led to a new positioning and new role for the audience, and (3) the efforts to multiply comedic forms as tools of criticism.

AN OVERVIEW OF THE PRODUCTION'S ARGUMENT

While several versions of the script of *1789* have been published (see Bibliography), none includes every textual moment, nor does the film (compiled from thirteen different evenings in June 1973) capture the entire piece. This would, in any case, be impossible, as improvisation was built into performance. Hence the production varied slightly from evening to evening and indeed evolved over the three-year performance period. Furthermore, the simultaneity of action created an experience that changed considerably depending on where audience members were located and where they concentrated their attention. Nevertheless, it can be asserted that the piece was successfully structured to say: "You have received one image of the French Revolution, but we are going to suggest another way of understanding what happened." Indeed, *1789* was conceived as a questioning of the founding myth of the French Republic with all theatrical elements tuned to contest the notion of "the victory of the French People," as well as to clarify the process underlying the formation of modern social classes in France.

One of the first sketches of *1789* brought to life a famous cartoon etching from the revolutionary period in which "the People" (represented as a donkey or beast of burden) rises up and bucks off the King, while keeping at bay "the Aristocracy" (a gander) and "the Clergy" (a crow). The message is clear: the People will no longer stand to be ridden. From that point on, however, through juxtaposition, characterization, careful editing of documentary material and other means, *1789* demonstrates that this iconography of the "victory of the People" obfuscates how the Revolution ushered in a new power structure in which the landholding bourgeoisie and professional classes replaced the monarchy, the nobility, and the clergy as rulers, leaving behind the rural and urban poor. Such an interpretation gives the lie to the myth of the revolutionary success of a unified "Third Estate" (often understood synonymously as "the People") or the 98 per cent of the population purportedly set equally on the path to liberty and fraternity after the celebrated taking of the Bastille on July 14, 1789.

This lesson builds on sketches loosely organized to follow the revolutionary events from Louis XVI's convocation of the Estates General (January 1789) to the sale of the Catholic Church's properties and goods (November 1789). It figures such key historical moments as the Tennis Court Oath; the storming by the Parisian populace of the political prison, the Bastille; the process of drafting the Declaration of the Rights of Man by the Constitutional Assembly; and the establishing of martial law and empowerment of a National Guard to keep order.

Internal commentary and criticism is affected by replaying the same event in two complementary ways, by juxtaposing radically different perspectives and by opposing contrary versions of the same situation. For example, to reinforce the centrality and crucial importance of the storming of the Bastille, actor/revolutionaries told in a 30-minute segment to small groups of audience members the story of the taking of the prison, after which a carnival show depicted the rationale for the events through illustrations of royal oppression (a game of targets and a wrestling match) and through a burlesque of the Comédie Française portraying the emigration of the King's brother, the Count d'Artois. This doubled segment illustrated both the empowerment of the Third Estate and the "People's" own pleasure in their newly recognized strength. Earlier, however, the impoverishment and hardships of the rural peasantry had been represented by a chilling sketch in which four fathers, placed around the playing space in kneeling position besides their wives and babies, strangled their children in order to put an end to their starvation. While the fathers wailed and the mothers stretched out their arms in a desperate search for some form of help, a resplendent King Louis XVI – one of many images of a feckless ruler – promenaded onto the playing area to Handel's *Royal Fireworks* music, blithely ignorant of the suffering around him. This type of juxtaposition, multiplied many times over, articulated the absence in the political arena of the concerns about and voices of the poorest people.

The real fate of the poor after the Revolution was again illustrated in a spaced replay of "the flight of King Louis and Queen Marie-Antoinette to Varennes." In the first moments of the play, the Royals, after Louis's failure to maintain foreign troops in France, sneak away in a melodramatic pantomime to supposed safety in Varennes; but a representative of "the People" victoriously unmasks them. In the second version, near the play's end, the King and Queen are protected by a group of bourgeois citizens, costumed in anticipation of the gaudy splendor of the new industrial class that will govern France after 1830. This reinterpretation supports the Marxist thesis orienting the production that the real beneficiary of the Revolution was the rising bourgeoisie.

To give an overall rhythm to the production, the string of vignettes lead to points of explosion (such as the contagiously happy celebration of the taking of the Bastille) or to points of halt, which underlie the near impossible quest for equality. Notably, in Part II, which follows the raucous Bastille celebration, each of the three times the *leitmotiv* "the Revolution is finished" is pronounced (in segments: "Two Episodes of the Celebration," "Parliamentary Debate," and "The Auction"), the actors freeze. At each junction, a self-impressed, recently tapped member of the emerging power structure (the National Guard, the Constitutional

Assembly, a Bourgeois Deputy), calls for "law and order" as means to stop the revolutionary process and the dreams of the working classes. The only stable character in the production – that is, the only character portrayed nonironically and consistently by one actor rather than by a host of actors, Marat – pronounces the play's democratic message at its close: "Citizens, what have we gained by destroying the aristocracy of the nobles, if it is replaced by the aristocracy of the wealthy" (p. 42) (see Figure 3.1).

COLLECTIVE CREATION

By the time the Théâtre du Soleil emerged in 1970 from its improvisational approach to *Les Clowns*, it had arrived at an understanding of what collective work should and should not be. Dissatisfied with the way *Les Clowns* atomized the group and emphasized individual talent, seeking a more direct way of commenting on the state of France after the shake-up of the events of May 68, the company (now twenty-six actors, fourteen technicians, and Ariane Mnouchkine) agreed to explore the French Revolution. Mnouchkine had suggested this topic because of its central place in the French imaginary and thus its place as part of the patrimony of all members of the company. The actors agreed that while they "knew" the Revolution, they really did not know it in detail or in its complexity: "The Revolution we learn about in primary school has become a kind of fairy tale that sticks in your memory as a series of Epinal images" (Mnouchkine and Penchenat 1971: 123). The Soleil set out to learn how the Revolution might have been stolen from the People.

They began by setting up study groups and attending lectures by Professor Elisabeth Brisson, contracted exclusively for them. They read classical political analysts, such as Alexis de Tocqueville and the historian Jules Michelet. But they also delved into more contemporary analyses of class struggle during the revolutionary period by Daniel Guérin, Albert Soboul, and Georges Lefebve. They read the revolutionary theorist and propagandist Marat, poured over the rich collection of political cartoons from the period, watched films on the French Revolution by Jean Renoir (*La Marseillaise*) and Abel Gance (*Napoleon*), as well as viewing Griffith's silent melodrama, the classic *Orphans in the Storm*. Nurtured and inspired by these images and perspectives, they began the process of collective improvisations at the Palais des Sports, an immense

Figure 3.1 The character Marat denounces the bourgeois National Assembly for putting an end to the Revolution, *1789*, 1971

sports arena in southwestern Paris. Mnouchkine divided the actors into five groups, which would be recomposed from time to time, each one working on one of the five platforms set up in a rectangular pattern (26 meters long by 14 meters wide) that was being developed as the playing area.

From the outset, a consensus had been reached that the company would create an environmental piece that could be moved from one basketball court to another, in anticipation of traveling throughout France. The Soleil wanted the work to have the popular aspect and excitement of a sporting event but also to recall the popular fairgrounds theater during the Revolutionary period. Mnouchkine's proposition accepted by all was that the actors would play eighteenth-century fair-ground players performing for a popular audience the events of the French Revolution. This choice immediately suggested an atmosphere and tone that would combine satire, farce, physical theater, caricature, and mime – harking back to performance traditions of open-air theater.

This "theater-in-the-theater" approach also afforded the Soleil another means and dimension of commentary. Actors frequently introduced sketches through a microphone – an anachronism suggesting that the criticism vested upon the protagonists of the Revolutionary drama could also be levied at contemporary power plays. Through the shifting temporal perspective and the multiplication of layers to each character-ization – that is, contemporary actors, acknowledged as such, performing itinerant open – air actors of the eighteenth century and performing constantly changing characters in the Revolutionary drama – the flesh and blood actors of the Soleil chastised the unsuccessful social revolu-tion of 1968. Their sketches about the Revolution of 1789 touched by analogy upon the failure of trade unions to seize the opportunity opened up by the May 68 revolt, the draconian rules imposed by the govern-ment to stop public meetings during the period, and the menacing force of the riot police.

At the beginning of each rehearsal, Mnouchkine would usually suggest the theme around which actors would improvise. As many as ten or fifteen fleshed-out sketches were proposed toward the end of each day; and these were critiqued by the entire group. Some were immediately thrown out. Most improvisations were eventually recombined. Sparked by the improvisations, Mnouchkine would generate more suggestions for improvisations for the next day. Bits of as many as seventeen sketches, culled from four months of improvisations from July to October 1970, would eventually make up a single segment of the dozen segments of the final production. Mnouchkine attended to the coherency of the approach, supervised the articulation between sketches, and fixed the final ordering of the segments. Sophie Lemasson, Mnouchkine's assistant, annotated each day the work deemed worthy of being kept. With actor Jean-Claude Penchenat, Lemasson also assembled the final text that served as the theater program.

The Soleil's improvisatory method meant that actors had to give up in the first phase any notion of owning a role or even an improvised moment – a moment that would often be slipped into another actor's repertory. On the other hand, because actors were personally in harmony politically and socially with their work, because they were committed to the play's lesson, they experienced little discomfort in terms of self-expression and performance. Furthermore, engaged as they were in the creation of their own costumes and make-up, in building the trestle tables on which they performed (even using authentic eighteenth-century carpentry techniques), and in cleaning up and painting the theater when they eventually moved into the Cartoucherie (September 1970), they lived fully within the collective sphere. Indeed, when they began improvisations for *1793*, the sequel to *1789*, they were so attuned to each others' skills that they could improvise in groups of twenty or more.

AUDIENCE INVOLVEMENT

Moving into the nineteenth-century Cartoucherie de Vincennes four months before the Parisian premier of *1789* was a form of poetic justice for the pugnacious Théâtre du Soleil. That this former armaments factory, once also an army barracks, should become the site of a theater company intent on decrying war and applauding the potential for social harmony also signaled the company's distance from other French theatrical institutions, most still located in **Italianate spaces**. Without performance rules, without hierarchical seating in place, without inscribed codes of audience conduct, a new playing space – and all that entails in terms of a new form of spectator – was ripe for invention. This freedom to create a new experience of theater, thanks to a completely undetermined space, has been a major spur to Mnouchkine's creativity ever since.

Already conceived for a sports arena, the scenographic design of *1789* fit readily into the vast second and third hangars of the cast iron, brick, and stone Cartoucherie structure. What had to be determined was how to position the audience in that space and how to utilize the first, or entrance hangar. In line with their goals of demystifying the process of both history and theater-making, Mnouchkine and members of the company turned the cavernous entrance into a combination exhibition space (on the French Revolution), welcome hall (for mingling and chatting between company and audience members), and orientation foyer to the work of the Soleil (presenting the history of the company and its costume collection). The front of the house was, in this way, partially shadowed by the backstage operations of theater-making, putting the public immediately into contact with theater work.

Spectators' involvement in the process continued in the combined second and third hangars, where they could converse with performers, watch them put on costumes and make-up, and ready themselves for performance. The dressing areas were located behind the five rectangular trestle tables that designated the playing area. Ushered into the combined hangar early – and with a lighting plan that illuminated brightly the whole area – the spectators had time to wander, look around, and take in not only the preparing actors but also the four towers from which the spot operators worked, located on the four corners of the rectangle formed by the trestle tables. The public could easily see also the extensive light grid suspended from the 20-foot high ceiling, and the light and sound boards located within the audience's spaces.

Spectators had also to decide where to position themselves, in what was one of the most remarked upon and exciting elements of this production. For *1789* offered two potential spaces to the audience: They could choose to sit on bleachers (about 800 places) to the left of the tables and looking down at the action, from which they could see the 5-feet high trestle platforms connected by walkways and rigged for backdrops. Or they could become part of the action by standing in the floor space in the middle of the platforms (about 200 places). This latter choice conferred upon the public the status of actor, as, depending on where a sketch was taking place, standing spectators had to rush from trestle table to table, jockeying for good viewing positions. They had to make way for the actor/characters who sometimes strode arrogantly through their midst, as did the "Constitutional Assembly delegates." They had to squeeze together to avoid clashes with the giant marionettes representing the King and Queen that were paraded through the audience by "the joyous women of Paris bringing the Royals back from Versailles." Standing spectators thus became, within the logic of the production, eighteenth-century fair spectators watching and responding to the Revolution played out before their eyes – their own status as actors confirmed by the seated audience watching them, as well as the company, "perform" (see Figure 3.2).

On only a few occasions was the house darkened to isolate, through spots, certain sketches. One instance was the harrowing infanticide, mentioned earlier, in which four peasant fathers on four different plat-forms strangled their starving babies. Such occasions threw the piece momentarily into a gripping melodramatic mode. Most of the time, however, the lighting encompassed and held together as one body – albeit with differing roles – audiences and actors, allowing for both identification with the group experience and the possibility of taking some distance from the action. Such distance was enhanced by the estranging devices incorporated into the performance: bowing after certain sketches; anachronistic microphones into which actors announced what they would perform in the next sketch; replaying, as discussed, from a different perspective the same scene.

This self-consciousness, fundamental to *1789*, was significantly chal-lenged only once. During the 30-minute "Storming of the Bastille" seg-ment, the most meaningful for the play's lesson and for the creative incorporation of the audience, a form of suturing took place. Each of the some forty members of the company drew to him or herself indi-vidual audiences from both the standing and seated publics. Each com-pany member, now a "character" who had "been there," narrated to increasing drum rolls the taking of the Bastille. Each of the groups – actors and spectators together – was ostensibly caught up in the momentous events of that July day, thrilling together to the voices rising in unison to proclaim: "And we took the Bastille. We took it!" (p. 30). Spectators willingly waltzed with a bear, chain danced, tossed rings, and applauded the acrobats and wrestlers celebrating the "People's victory" in the following street festival segment. When the first haughty and violent declaration of the "end of the Revolution" by General Lafayette of the National Guard put a sudden and unexpected stop to this adrenaline rush, the Soleil's point about who really won the Revolution was introduced with brio.

Audiences of *1789* were so hooked on the show that they had difficulty leaving the theater at the end of the performance. In fact, when the com-pany performed free after the first six months, 2,000 spectators showed up

Figure 3.2 The Théâtre du Soleil performs *1789* on elevated platform or trestle tables, with the audience incorporated into the performance, 1971

and the performance spilled out into the park in front of the theater, lasting well into the night. *1789* struck a chord that resonated with the political moment: The production spoke deeply to a particular generation about its most serious questions. It was both a celebration and an exorcism.

MULTIPLICATION OF COMEDIC AND OTHER FORMS

Peter Brook's concept of "rough theatre" comes to mind when describing *1789*: a very broad, physically based comedy meant to shake up and critique the status quo. The production indeed echoed such "rough" celebrations as the formerly well-attended and socially all-encompassing Fête de l'Humanité, the French Communist Party's annual fair, a civic outing that bestows upon the public a role of good fun, playfulness, and carnivalesque behavior – at once subversive and contained. However, *1789* was a good deal more complicated than a pastiche or parody of political or cultural power, although it was that too.

Within the conceit of the theatrical ***mise-en-abime*** (actors playing actors playing characters), the production also brilliantly reviewed popular theater forms, ranging from storytelling (the frame) to melodrama, ***commedia dell'arte***, guignol, silent film, slapstick, mime, cabaret, and even circus tricks. Frequently coupled, such as the silent film *cum* striptease sketch of the Aristocrats' renouncement of their privileges ("The Night of 4 August"), these dizzyingly merging forms demonstrated Mnouchkine's and the Théâtre du Soleil's extreme virtuosity and concern to keep the audience engaged, stimulated, and in a state of high expectation. In one such instance, "The Call for Petitions to the King," a fairground actor become town crier, in direct address to the audience, transforms himself into the second of three successive petitioners to express his needs. The first, a peasant, in a farcical mode, had earlier proclaimed that she wanted to write against the salt tax. But she failed because of not knowing how to form an "s" – even after having plucked for use as a pen, in an energetic mime, a feather from a chicken. The second petitioner, who can draw if not write, then portrays in *commedia* gestures a self-satisfied and wilier peasant hoping to show the king that his cow is lonely: He draws two happy cows. His petition is, however, also a failure, as the food-chain of petitioners (more variations on *commedia* schemers) continue devouring the previous petition – until a bourgeois deputy stops the movement: His petition will reach the King.

This segment was followed immediately by a classic guignol, with puppeteers running through the audience to set their stage for a puppet show lampooning the power structure in which "Marie-Antoinette" conducts herself as an aggressive, unpredictable "Judy" and "Louis XVI" as an unbridled, if henpecked, "Punch." The height of theater-in-the theater layering occurred near the end of the performance in which the fair actors (in a fantastic leap forward) play infantilized nineteenth-century bourgeois arrivistes watching with fear and then delight another guignol (with human marionettes this time) performing a vignette of the ultimate defeat of the "People." Such rapidly changing and physically demanding performance modes kept spectators alert and energized, dazzled by the display of irrepressible talent.

To the complex mixture of forms and internal commentary, Mnouchkine added a documentary element that grew in importance in the production's second half. By selectively incorporating actual texts from the Constitutional Assembly, especially those focusing on the Declaration of the Rights of Man, *1789* commented on the constraints in thinking that prevented delegates from seeing lower classes as equals. In a particularly disturbing sketch following a historic assembly debate on the right to property that determined that "Inequality is [...] natural" (p. 30), fair comedians playing plantation owners in the colony of Santo Domingo (now Haiti) rejoice that Blacks are "property" and not "men." The juxtaposition of this illustrative sketch with the preceding historical debate drove home the message about the insularity and self-serving policy-making of the bourgeois deputies.

1789 AND RELATED THEATER PIECES

"Rough" theater, *1789*, can also be characterized as part of the environmental theater movement that reached a peak in the 1960s and 1970s. Environmental theater refuses the division between audience and actors, stressing the creation of a receptive community. Theater-makers, from American Richard Schechner and his Performance Group to Italian Luca Ronconi with his 1970 production of *Orlando Furioso*, thereby designed theatrical experiences that depended on the audience's active, physical participation. Such projects, as we have seen with Mnouchkine's, called on the spectators' willingness to engage with, even absorb, the materiality of the theatrical work, accepting its more obvious theatricality but also experiencing its greater physical reality and more explicit sensuality.

We can also place the work within the many collective denunciations of injustice, such as Le Théâtre de l'Aquarium's satire of real-estate development in the heart of Paris, *Marchands de Ville* [Selling the City] (1972), that filled French theaters in the 1970s. Mnouchkine herself credits certain forms of collective street theater as inspiring her work, notably the efforts of the **Bread and Puppet Theater**, and especially their *Cry of the People For Meat*. She saw the production in Paris in 1969 and took from this experience, as an undergirding for *1789*, the company's highly poetic and oversized imagery and especially the piece's earnest and joyous intensity. The Bread and Puppet's commitment to a street theater of both beauty and fiery political militancy and to a collective of artists and thinkers undoubtedly helped reinforce Mnouchkine's sense that she, also, could be a player in the political debates of her times.

1789 launched the international reputation of the Théâtre du Soleil – and encouraged the creation of other theatrical collectives, such as the bilingual Jeune Lune Company of Minneapolis, Minnesota in the United States. It confirmed Mnouchkine's belief in collective work and in participatory audiences. It was also the apogee of Mnouchkine's experimentation with rough and tumble self-conscious forms of farce and parody, forms that made *1789* a theatrical echo of the social and political contestation out of which it grew. In most of her later productions, and especially since 1980, Mnouchkine has approached history obliquely and without the constant shifting of styles characteristic of *1789*. This change in orientation has given to her later work a distinctive iconographic – we might even say ritualistic – coloration.

RICHARD II: MYTHIC STORYTELLING, HYBRIDIZING ASIA, AND GEOMETRIZING POWER

Created in 1981, Mnouchkine's *Richard II* won French theater's "Grand Prix" for best production (1982). Performed in tandem with two other Shakespearian works (*Twelfth Night* and *Henry IV, Part 1*) of a projected but never realized six-part Shakespeare Cycle, *Richard II* was the kind of production that caused spectators at the **Avignon Festival** in 1982 and later at the Los Angeles Olympic Arts Festival, where it toured in 1984, to admit that experiencing Mnouchkine's Shakespeares had metaphorically changed their lives – its shimmering opulence and entirely original formal aesthetic subjugating them (Quillet 1999: 88).

After years of collective exploration and devising texts, Mnouchkine had returned to Shakespeare because she wanted to grapple with strong, dramatic architecture. She had a notion to build a single dramatic universe with certain gestures and character types appearing from one play to the next. She also had, at that point, a company with several exceptionally charismatic actors, physically and intellectually ripe to take on demanding Shakespearian roles, as well as an athletic host of younger actors recently culled from one of her intensive mask workshops. Finally, she sought out Shakespeare in order to delve into how his theater handles history, in an effort to prepare herself for what she hoped would be her own next phase of historical work.

Typically, she was unsure of what form the work would take when rehearsals began. However, after a viewing of Kurosawa's epic film, *Kagemusha*, she saw the traces of the direction she wanted to follow: an emphasis on corporeal iconography and inscribed social codes, and a look and feel that would recall samurai warrior culture and Asian performance traditions, particularly **kabuki**, **Noh**, and **Balinese dance**. She accordingly had the actors study samurai films and also the landscapes of the vast Mongolian steppes, in order to help them interiorize a sense of expansiveness. She set up a rigorous physical training schedule that included running 5 miles a day, paying close attention to nutrition, and taking lessons on projection from a vocal coach. The result was a production in which dramatic storytelling took on a mythic or ritual hue, based as it was in a tightly choreographed amalgam and reinvention of traditional Asian theater forms. The movement patterns that Mnouchkine imagined for *Richard II* etched on stage the functioning of power.

THE WORK OF MYTHIC STORYTELLING

Shakespeare's *Richard II*, like all his history plays, stages the history of medieval England, while also examining the complex emotional and psychological make-up of those to whom power falls and those who struggle to attain it. A more metaphorical reading of the play allows one to see how such stories of desire, struggle, winning, and losing – of the passing of time and of cyclical moments – also delve into the meaning of human life, a questioning both timeless and inescapable. King Richard himself recognizes the vanity of striving for power when death hovers always in the background, keeping "court," and "grinning at [the] pomp" (III: 2 lines 160–3). Any director who tackles the rich interpretive possibilities of *Richard II* has to decide how to read this history play, where to put the emphasis that will speak to his or her audience, and how to save the production from becoming a museum piece, in which "what has always been done" gets done again.

Richard II invites explorations into the eponymous protagonist's vacillations between seemingly paranoid violence and lucid existentialism, between true patriotism and heartless imperialism, between passionate belief in his own divine right and shameful anguish at his overturning. By turns charming, sly, magnificent, brutal, mystical, ambiguous, suicidal, Richard would seem to evolve into his own jester, perhaps a victim of flatterers, perhaps not a victim at all. Like Bolingbroke, his arch rival and eventual conqueror, Richard may be read as complex and conflicted, a young ruler invested in power, while on the brink of recognizing the foolishness of mortal triumph – an almost wise, possibly Christic figure. Theater people have been attracted to this play precisely to respond to the enigma of Richard and to that of his successor, Bolingbroke, who combines a sweet temperament with an unquenchable thirst for control.

In directing *Richard II* in 1981, Mnouchkine had little competition from the ghosts of past French productions, the last staging of *Richard* having been done by Jean Vilar in 1947. Nevertheless, Shakespeare, with Chekov and Molière, has been since 1960 among the most frequently performed playwrights in France. There are, then, certain preconceptions about how Shakespeare should be done, and especially a tendency to favor the sinister obsessive vision prevalent in France thanks to the popularization of Jan Kott's psychoanalytical study, *Shakespeare, our Contemporary* (1964) – a vision that had, in fact, informed Mnouchkine's first unsettling Shakespearian production, *A Midsummer Night's Dream* (1968) (and that certainly nuanced, among other productions, **Patrice Chéreau**'s remarkable readings of Marivaux in the 1970s and 1980s.)

By the time of *Richard II*, however, Mnouchkine's aesthetic had moved away from the compelling eroticism of her early Shakespearian work. Committed to physical theater – including seeing her actors as a choral body – intrigued by the call of social and political systems, repulsed by psychological realism that explores individual motives of characters to the detriment of a larger allegorical lesson, Mnouchkine refused the temptation to plumb the murky psyches of the two kings. She chose to see the play primarily as a series of confrontations in which feudal aristocrats plot against each other – with Richard and Bolingbroke occasionally reflecting upon what happens as a result of such machinations. In keeping with her general directorial orientation, she set aside psychological probing to construct a lush pageant of raw ruling power at work, concentrating on how the newly powerful replace the formerly powerful in a cycle of cruelty, aggression, and coercion destined to be repeated *ad infinitum*.

She took upon herself the translation and adaptation of the text, clarifying the Shakespearian language in free unrimed verse that communicates easily the negotiations of the courtiers and the strategies of Richard, Bolingbroke, and their supporters. She also frequently cut what might be considered redundant lines or moments (e.g. the Welsh encampment II: 4) to strengthen and intensify Bolingbroke's drive toward destruction-tinged victory. She eliminated almost entirely the subplot of Aumerle's family drama (V: 2), omitting the scene in which his father, the Duke of York, angrily discovers the latest scheme against Bolingbroke, now the new King Henry IV. By cutting also the sentimental groom who visits Richard in his last prison (V: 5), Mnouchkine focused attention in the last moments of the production on Bolingbroke's reaction to the assassinated King Richard, setting up a parallel between their two destinies.

Following Shakespeare's lead, we might easily subtitle Mnouchkine's production "a ritual of wrath-kindled gentlemen" (I: 1, line 151): For urgency, anxiety, and electricity characterized the staging and conferred, as Adrian Kiernander has remarked, an almost "hysterical intensity" on the perfectly balanced stage pictures and martial formations (Kiernander 1993: 113). To understand more precisely how Mnouchkine gave shape to this ritualized vision of *Richard II*, we will examine the production's iconography, scenography, and choreography, paying particular attention to how Asia figures in the work and how elements of theater – especially movement patterns – created an allegory of power.

A HYBRID ASIA

Much has been made of Mnouchkine's borrowing and blending of Asian elements and theatrical techniques in her Shakespeare Cycle, including her displacing the referential real of *Richard II* to a fantastical medieval Japan. From our perspective, the central and most important aspect of this turn to Asia in *Richard II* was the latitude it afforded her to create the feeling of staged ritual. Mnouchkine took from Asian theater a model that allowed her to perfect a gestic system and clarify physical lines. She refined and defined – with her actors and designers – set and costumes and a network of signs in order to offer an onstage lesson. Her precision staging so transcended the ordinary that it attained the luminous power of the sacred – the sacred indeed being the impetus behind all traditional Asian performance styles.

For *Richard II*, the stage, as in Noh, kabuki, and Balinese traditions, was a large, empty space – occupying the 14 × 14 square meters favored by Mnouchkine and her set designer, Guy-Claude François. The playing area was covered by hemp matting and flanked by two runways from which the actors could rush on and off, as in kabuki and Noh. Its emptiness conjured up a world both past and present. As in kabuki, small striped tents on the runways provided spaces for costume changes and for regrouping actors for entrances. Seven black vertical lines divided the playing space into eight 2-meter horizontal sectors, each sector bordering and containing the movements of individual characters during scenes of confrontation or judgment (see Figure 3.3).

The color scheme, like that of Japanese lacquered boxes, favored red, black, white, and gold. The lavish costumes, in rich variations of these hues, caught and reflected the light easily: They were made of highly textured ecclesiastical cloth and combined many layers – some of which floated and shimmered with the constant movement of the actors. A collage of long-skirted kimono, Elizabethan ruff and doublet, samurai head piece, and curved scimitar, each costume also communicated something of the temperament or position of the character. Richard – triumphant king – was all in white; Bolingbroke – on the way to kingship – threw off his black and gold raiment for one of white and gold. Sculpted white-face make-up for the younger characters (as in Noh) aided in the transformation of actors into signs, with red shadings under eyes, on cheeks and chins, and the side of the nose adding notes of anger or spleen. The older characters (Gaunt, York, Lady Glouscester) wore kabuki-inspired masks, demarcating them as a generation having already succumbed to the onslaught of the new power politics.

Stage-helpers, costumed in black tunics, pants, and head gear (reminiscent of *koken* in Japanese **bunraku**) unostentatiously slipped on and off stage, placing and removing the few iconic set pieces. They also carried out the dead and held up the backdrops when entrances were made

Figure 3.3 The character King Richard II, surrounded by courtiers in Mnouchkine's kabuki-inspired production of Shakespeare's *Richard II*, 1982

from back stage and not from the ramps. In contrast, the colorful, red-nosed, red-legged clowns occupied noisily the whole space of the playing area when it became the Queen's garden. They bemoaned comically Richard's fate, as the Queen hid behind branches held up to her face by discrete stage helpers.

The set pieces, few in number, often lacquered in black, recalled Asian designs and bore significant symbolic weight: A low table was both Richard's throne and his funeral bier; a black jungle gym pagoda – the tower sheltering him, a tower Richard scaled like a monkey in a cage; the prison – another cage – made of thin white rods was Richard's execution chamber. In only a loin cloth and wrist bracelets, the humbled Richard meets his death, slowly falling to the cage floor with the waning sound of the wrist bells jingling mournfully. This is all we hear in the only blackout of the production. (Lighting, in general, varied with the action but remained basically warm and dreamy, seeping through the tented ceiling or glowing from the Japanese-style footlights.)

Perhaps, the most pregnant markers of the spectrally beautiful production – Asian-inspired as well – were the 14 × 14 square meter superposed backdrops, eleven in all, each rigged to fall at the end of a segment. Not only did these silken hangings establish structure by floating down to end a moment, but they also mimicked and exteriorized Richard's mood and suggested a cycle of rising and falling power. Golden at the beginning – with a celestial globe figured in Jackson Pollack-like drips of white and red – deep red during the mutual accusations of treason by Mowbray and Bolingbroke, the drop was black with a silver moon for Richard's assassination. Earlier, when power was passed to Bolingbroke, the virgin king, the drop, as was his costume, was white with a golden sun. These drops, as economical as a Japanese pen and ink drawing in which the mere outline of a crane can suggest long life, helped place Mnouchkine's interpretation of Richard within a cosmic vision. They hinted at how the universe endures, all in being seasoned by the individual's passions and destiny.

GEOMETRIZING POWER

We have seen how the material elements of *Richard II* contribute to an Asian feel and to what we might call an Asian-inspired aesthetic goal: that is, the linking together, through potent signs, of different levels of existence, or the transcending of the here and now by giving form to the invisible and the abstract. Perhaps the most powerful aspects of Mnouchkine's *Richard II* in conveying the abstract (in this case the workings of power, the rage to obtain it, and the final insanity of the chase), were the choreography and movement patterns. Mnouchkine's vision was further enhanced by what, at that point in her career, was a radical departure in the use of music.

In Mnouchkine's staging of *Richard II* the actors hardly ever stood still. Connected to the earth as in kabuki, the actors – when not running or prancing – glided across the stage in semi-squat position, adjusting their movements to cues from the onstage musicians. For this production, Jean-Jacques Lemêtre, at that point the new musical director, assembled some 300 percussion and drone instruments for his off-side orchestral space. He kept the beat, punctuated the movements, and created musical themes for the principal characters. Rather than a symphonic underscoring as in prior productions, the music thus helped transform the actors into dancing forms. Their constant up and down movement and exaggerated sighing or swooning created the illusion of an onstage, intensely connected breathing organism, an organism fully cognizant of the location of power.

Hence, only Richard occupied center stage – until Bolingbroke took over. In Act I: 1, for example, the nobles rushed onstage in a spiral, positioning themselves as on a chess board, with King Richard in the middle. During his questioning of Bolingbroke and Mowbray, these courtiers, horizontally surrounding Richard, punctuated his speeches by movements and gestures signaling emotional leaps. Each courtier had his own set of striking or cocking motions, timed to make the whole pattern look like a highly regulated human machine, with King Richard as the energy source.

For the precisely choreographed entrances, aristocratic courtiers, summoned by a gong, rushed onstage in a pack: During the battle scenes they resembled a troupe of centaurs (especially notable in III: 3). Stomping, snorting, trying to hold the line, the characters – half men, half horses, hit their thighs with riding crops. They projected stunning visions of military energy and battle passion, their voices pitched to the music, spitting out words at the audience. Aligned in spatial zones, they bumped into each other, foreseeing their own struggles for power to come – with Henry Percy, foreshadowing Henry IV, completely unable to control his horse from breaking rank.

The final composition – the staging of Richard's death – found Bolingbroke alone holding the broken Richard in his arms. He then placed him on the floor under the throne/bier on which he himself stretched out, taking the exact position of Richard's corpse. In this doubled funeral portrait, Mnouchkine portrayed as enduringly as the brass rubbings in Westminster Abbey the ultimate absurdity of the struggle to the heights.

RICHARD II AMIDST OTHER CONTEMPORARY SHAKESPEARES

The cues taken from kabuki and Noh theater and from the dancing bodies of Balinese performance helped Mnouchkine devise for *Richard II* an aesthetic of such rigor, but also such unfamiliar and compelling force, that many critics speak of the experience as transporting. *Richard II* managed to realize a condensation of universes: at once mystical and material, strange and familiar, theatrical and grandly human. Mnouchkine's production of *Richard II* thus conveyed us to that other pole of theater theorized by Peter Brook: the holy, in which a certain formal sensibility and aesthetic virtuosity creates an exceptional communal experience, thereby proffering a sense of the divine and imbuing the public with positive energy, while transforming the actors into conduits of morality.

This is quite another realm than that to which other recent celebrated contemporary French productions of Shakespeare have taken us. Mnouchkine's heightened and drawn-out metaphors, for instance, distanced themselves from Peter Brook's own stripped-down versions of *The Tempest* (1990) or *Hamlet* (2003). In both, while practicing the seamless movement from scene to scene and iconic simplicity characteristic of all his works, Brook foregrounded through his casting his multicultural acting community with their particular acting quirks. He also joyfully played with the tortured psychology of his protagonists. His goal – like Mnouchkine's to unite – includes also, as hers does not, a dose of deconstructive self-reflection. Brook is still asking from within his Shakespearian productions how theater can mean in a world so saturated with meaning systems that meaning seems to be lost.

L'INDIADE OU L'INDE DE LEURS RÊVES: THE CIXOUSIAN PARTNERSHIP, AESTHETICS OF THE HYPER-REAL, AND BORDER CROSSERS

L'Indiade (1987), subtitled "the India of their dreams," is the second text written specifically for Mnouchkine and the Théâtre du Soleil by

Hélène Cixous. Like the first, her 1985 *Sihanouk (The Terrible but Unfinished Story of Norodom Sihanouk, King of Cambodia)*, whose production culminated in another major prize for the company (Prix Europe, Taormina 1986), this piece employs the recent history of the Asian continent as means to explore and image a pressing and ever-threatening world political situation. Here, the focus is on civil war and genocide, targeting for the larger allegory the independence and subsequent bloody partitioning of India. As in all of Mnouchkine's and Cixous' work, "Asia is [thus] not Asia. It is theatre Asia [. . .], another world, a second world [. . .], a reservoir, a gigantic cavern of images" (Prenowitz 2004: 19). It is consequently a place where archaic desires can be played out and examined. However, in this production, contrary to *Richard II*, the dream of Asia did not give rise to a hybridity of Asian forms, but rather to a rendering of Asia in such heightened realism that characters seemed both life-like and cartoonish – "real" Indians paradoxically haunting a symbolic stage.

An epic theatrical journey alluding to Homer, 5-hours long, with forty-nine characters hastening on and offstage, *l'Indiade* rehearses the fears and prejudices but also the bid for self-determination and love that intertwined in the immensely painful and still volatile dual birthing of India and Pakistan. The play roughly follows the historical period from 1937 to 1948 and depicts the liberation and also dismembering of Britain's former colony, despite the dreams of unity of Mahatma Gandhi and Jawarharlal Nehru and their Congress Party – but in keeping with the more ferocious reverie of Mohammed Ali Jinnah. Leader and strategist of the Muslim league, Jinnah directs his fury at the inequality of Muslims, a perception which casts Gandhi's dream as a foolish nightmare: "In Indian country," says Jinnah's colleague Iqbal, "the table is not round" (p. 33). All these politicians dream a different India and they do so in debates among themselves and with the British colonial rulers. We hear also more colorful arguments about "India" from untouchable rickshaw drivers, ordinary soldiers, and peasants. "India" is also imagined in the lyrical musings of Gandhi, the theoretician of nonviolence, and in the pithy commentary of the Bengali pilgrim Haridasi, who bridges all the dreamers by her wandering.

To elaborate *her* dream of India, Cixous traveled there, immersing herself in Indian literature and history – a process that helped her decide that Mnouchkine's first idea of forging a play around the leadership and assassination of Indira Gandhi would not work. She felt that the story of the first female leader of India could not capture the passion of the new nations emerging and taking shape: Indira Gandhi did not speak to the passage from colonial to postcolonial with all its complexities. Cixous needed central characters with the charisma and panache of Norodom Sihanouk, the mythic figure of her first epic play for Mnouchkine. Her goal, consistent in all her theater work, was to find and confront "the angel" and "the beast" in the human heart (p. 25).

She thus sought material that could take on the ritualized form we have seen in *Richard II*. She wanted to be able to place onstage, as in *Sihanouk*, the multifaceted, multilayered universe of a Shakespearian drama, with its potential for helping make sense of reality and with its capacity to include characters from all walks of life making leaps in time and space. She therefore latched onto the metaphoricity of the "knights of the Congress Party" (p. 15). Through them, she sought to teach her audience about Gandhi's ideal of love:

> There's no love without fear. And yes, sometimes, no love without a kind of disgust, even repulsion. We human beings, Hindus, Muslims, men, women, we're so different, so strange. [. . .] If there are two leaves on a tree, they aren't identical but they do dance to the same breeze – that's true of the human tree too. Let's allow time for human affairs to grow and ripen.
>
> (Cixous 1987: 81–2)

Cixous wished to oppose this ideal to the West's concentration on hate, embroiled as it was in the Second World War during the same period.

Gandhi – with his generosity and acceptance of the other – represented for Cixous a choice maternal figure, a Solomonic good mother in keeping with the Cixousian definition of "the feminine." His ability to partner the world, to give unselfishly of himself, and to metamorphose, if necessary, in order to make space for a fuller community also merged with Cixous' notion of what theater should be and with what she saw Mnouchkine's theater work and Mnouchkine herself incarnating. She indeed figures this conjuncture in *Le Livre de Promethea*, her tribute to the director: "[How curious it is that] my so pretty, so clever, so theoretical theories are now embodied by reality in the person of Promethea [Ariane Mnouchkine] herself" (Cixous 1983: 12). Cixous' and Mnouchkine's complementarity resulted in a production that both kept the *theatrum mundi* aspects of a Shakespearian play while introducing original and compelling theatrical elements – notably hyper-real and "border-crossing" characters that contributed to the invention of a new and troubling aesthetic.

THE AESTHETIC CONTINUUM

The debt to Shakespeare in the fashioning of Cixous' play is alluded to in one of *l'Indiade*'s more elegiac passages. Lord Mountbatten, who comes to orchestrate Indian independence, recognizes the portentous nature of the event by referencing the bard's theater: "It's on such nights that in Shakespeare's plays, condemned lovers would kiss. On such nights, kings felt defeat approaching and queens sensed death's arrival" (p. 147). In the play's amplified sense of moment, in its oscillation between historical event and individual tragedy, in the range of characters and linguistic registers which establish collective and individual levels of plot, in the juxtaposition of moods and temporal shifts, and in its chains of metaphors, we do, indeed, see something of Shakespeare in *l'Indiade*. In production, we see especially how Mnouchkine, in the effort to convey meaning, as she did in her reading of *Richard II*, emphasized the possibilities lodged in the Shakespearian universe of invigorating physical work and intensely focused choreography and of ritualized and highly symbolic spaces.

In Mnouchkine's staging, for example, Gandhi, the soul of the production, was never alone. Always accompanied, including by the specter of his dead wife, Kastourbai, he was prolonged in the bodies of those listening and touching him and by his theme music, composed to represent his sweetness and played by Jean-Jacques Lemêtre – positioned side-stage left within a Calderesque assemblage of some 100 musical instruments. Gandhi's spirit infused the production, just as his always stage-center pleadings with Jinnah, or arguments with Nehru, or friendship duets with the Pathan, Badshah Khan, marked the emotional summits of the piece. In contrast to Gandhi's physical and emotional centrality, each time the two opposing camps (The Congress Party and the Muslim League) met, they – in their all-white formal dress – occupied strictly delineated segments of the vast 14 × 14 square meter stage, each seated on separate carpets spread over the off-white marble floor by the "people" of India. Tinged by the melodramatic use of music, especially the "monsoon wind" to denote crisis, the production seemed to say that the rigid Hindi and Muslim politicians were destined to never meld into one (see Figure 3.4).

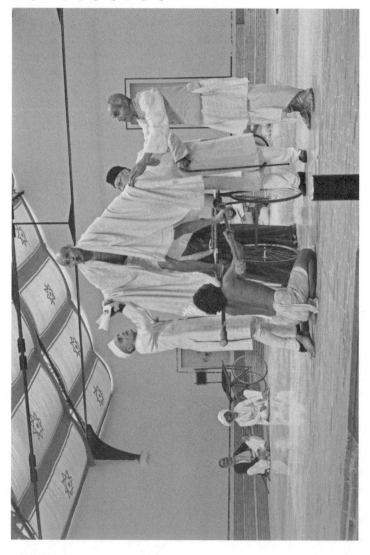

Figure 3.4 The character Gandhi pleads for peace, surrounded by members of the Congress Party and by his untouchable rickshaw driver, *l'Indiade*, 1987

The "people," on the other hand, formed an always energized, always moving vibrant mass, affecting the set changes, pulling and parading the leaders through the streets of Delhi in ochre rickshaws, confronting each other noisily and increasingly violently in quarrels marred by ethnic pride and dreams of vengeance. They flowed up onto the playing space out of the vomitorium located under the bleachers facing the stage, as though propelled by a nightmare they did not control. In the last and most startling of the three rickshaw parades, which created peaks of concentrated energy between political debates or Gandhi's strategizing, rickshaw drivers dragged piles of undifferentiated corpses across the stage – Muslims, Hindus, Sikhs, young, and old – in an apocalyptic vision of what civil war had wrought. This "united" India ironically commented on the failure of tolerance and the tenacity of Jinnah's fundamentalist claims.

From the urban sites of Bombay and New Delhi to the Punjab and Bengal and the mountainous borderlands between India and Afghanistan, the fictional places changed, but the physical space remained essentially the same, permeated by the warring dreams of India. As in *Richard II*, light was filtered from behind a gauze ceiling covering. "Doors," which permitted entrances from outside the dream-like space, demarcated the magnificent upstage expanse of brick-bordered marble. From "outside," the heroes of history entered to take the political decisions which determined the people's fate. Inside, the common characters were linked in swirling movement, by a constant musical underscoring, and through the witnessing and physical commentary of those people positioned on the brick borders. This vivid presence of a choral body: actors linked to each other as part of a many-headed, living, breathing organism – as already seen in the centaur scenes in *Richard II* (and later perfected in the choral groups of *The House of Atreus Cycle*, 1990–2) – externalized the emotional pulse of the community.

INFLECTIONS: HYPER-REALITY
AND BORDER-CROSSERS

In the aesthetic invented by Mnouchkine for *l'Indiade*, the uncanny creation of an Indian world that confused the boundaries between theater and the "real" established a major difference from prior productions. From the moment the public entered the entrance hangar of the theater space, the smell of curry and Indian spices overwhelmed the senses. "Indians" (actors dressed and made-up to resemble the characters they played, based on observations made during their preparatory travels to the subcontinent), milled about smiling or selling sweetmeats and pastries from a cart. They would later sell food at intermission. Haridasi, the Bengali pilgrim improvising in Indian English, asked for names: "Who are you, please?". She introduced spectators to each other, greeting them like old friends and telling her own story, wondering: "Do you believe in God?" "Do you know what is happening in India?" (Miller production notes, October 1987).

When the public moved into the next hangar to take its place, "Indians" were sweeping and dusting the playing space. They helped spectators to their seats, shyly making eye contact with individual members of the audience, while Haridasi chatted about the confrontation to come. She would later usher in the second-half of the production with news of the massacres of some 5,000 Hindus and Muslims. Other "Indians" muddied the boundaries of this performance of "Indianness." These were the actors visible in their open dressing-room space under the bleachers, putting the final touches on make-up and coiffing themselves in golden or red-orange turbans or skull-caps, clearly in the act of becoming characters. Many spectators thus experienced the "schizo-phrenia" of knowing and not knowing that they were in the theater, positioned both as European interlopers or tourists ready to be taken on a voyage and as audience members complicit with a theatrical project of transformation (Quillet 1999: 64).

The constant presence of Haridasi, storyteller, commentator, and witness, added yet another disconcerting layer to the performance, as she, border-crosser par excellence, spoke directly and throughout the play to the spectators – not as an actor of the company, but as a pilgrim on the same educational journey as the audience, as, indeed, its onstage partner (see Figure 3.5). At the same time, she occupied, in a logical impossibility, all the fictional places in the play, being present for the debates of great and small, conversing with the Mahatma, dismissing Gandhi's assassin as a "nothing" (p. 188) and responding, in the audience's place, to Gandhi's immortality: "He is *not* dead" (p. 190).

Haridasi's role as border-crosser was reinforced by yet another wanderer, Moona Baloo, a performed and performing female bear whose destiny in the production paralleled India's. When she became contaminated by the violence all around her, she struck out – killing the guardian of the Muslim temple, hurting her trainer, and revealing the beast in the human heart. Mnouchkine made her reverberate with all

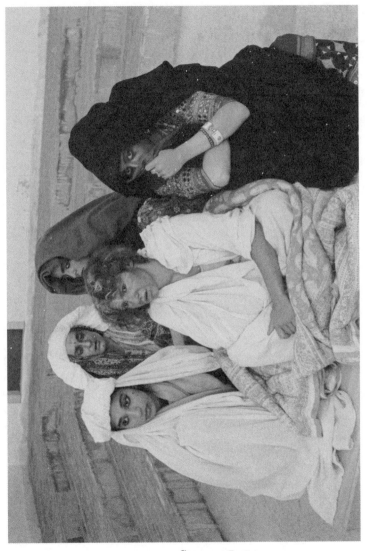

Figure 3.5 The character Haridasi (middle figure), the Bengali pilgrim, and other Indian women listen to the debate between members of the Congress Party and the Muslim League, *l'Indiade*, 1987

the anger around her, only calming down in the presence of Gandhi whose innocence she echoed and parodied. Killed, like Gandhi, Moona Baloo also can be read as a sacrificial victim. The presence of the bear, like that of Haridasi, linked the audience to yet another level of meaning, resonating with the generalized message of love. Moona Baloo pushed the production to a more enchanting level than that of the encounter with the hyper-real "Indians," whose gestures and detailed costuming both signaled the "real" and the Théâtre du Soleil's efforts to construct it.

NOSTALGIA FOR LOVE

As of all her plays, Cixous speaks of this one as offering a balm to existentialist angst through its ability to connect the here and now with the cosmos. Theater has long been for her a laboratory for living differently, for projecting alternative structures to the violence of the everyday, a "world that can tear itself away from the world as it is by becoming the sublime form of the world as it is" (Prenowitz 2004: 41). Gandhi, both wise and childlike, and his alter ego, the wondrous dancing bear, were meant to enliven this utopian vision and communicate the requisite mystery to capture the public's fantasy, to bind them to a common faith. Nevertheless, the force of Mnouchkine's staging of their devastating assassinations, combined with the 20-minute parade of corpses, situated as they were at play's end, rather than shoring up belief in the possibilities of life, tended to confirm the cataclysmic fragility of the veneer of civilization. It is as if Mnouchkine's gift for staging grand guignolesque melodrama and her explicit emphasis on people becoming killing machines undercut and put into question Cixous' message of love.

L'Indiade and contemporary epic theater

L'Indiade can be compared with Peter Brook's monumental epic production, The Mahabharata, Jean-Claude Carrière's adaptation of the sacred text of Hinduism. Created within the same period of time (1987), The Mahabharata, an 8-hour extravaganza, did not shirk from a vision of life that includes war and avarice as part of an un-erasable reality. Brook's work showed no nostalgia for a lost paradise but rather celebrated life with all its complications. Furthermore, Brook required his actors to claim and make their autonomy felt within the overall concept of the production. The site of emanation, theater, "came" from them.

They did not function primarily as another aspect of a total aesthetic concept, of a dream of India. This personalization added a dimension to Brook's work that Mnouchkine's actors, for the most part, did not and were not meant to attain.

DRUMS ON THE DAM: IN THE FORM OF AN ANCIENT PUPPET PLAY, PERFORMED BY ACTORS: THEATRICAL SELF-QUESTIONING AND THE ACTOR AS PUPPET

In *Drums on the Dam: In the Form of an Ancient Puppet Play, Performed by Actors*, Mnouchkine created with her actors a replica or a fantasy of bunraku puppet theater which enclosed a second puppet theater – setting up an allegory encompassing puppetry and life. This 1999 collaboration with Hélène Cixous took the total body mask work with her actors in *l'Indiade* to new heights and also broadened and layered her theatrical questioning. For in this production, Mnouchkine and Cixous skewer the power and greed that inform the crucial life and death decisions determining the future of human kind and also ask how theater dare speak about life. They thus affirm their political agenda, focusing in particular on an imperiled earth. But they also wonder, through the marionette form of the piece and its embedded allegory, to what extent theater is not merely a game of shadows. In its mimicry of action, is not theater a display or echo of how life works, with forces outside of most people's ken determining the truly earth-shattering decisions that kill off life and theater at the same time? Within Mnouchkine's never-ending theatrical meditation on the functioning of democracy, *Drums on the Dam* is her most pessimistic production and also her most beautiful – a voyage, a meditation, a revelation, and an accusation. It won the admiration of the bunraku and kabuki masters who attended performances in Japan in 2001, seeing in this production the poignancy and yearning of much of Japanese art (personal communication from Charles-Henri Bradier, June 2005).

ON THE PLAY'S ARGUMENT: INFLUENCES AND INTERPRETATIONS

Hélène Cixous found the inspiration for her story of self-interest and greed in an ancient Chinese tale. She looked for her aesthetic to Noh master, **Zeami**, whom she admires for his ability to condense and at the same time expand a play's universe. Inspired by Zeami, she crafted a timeless fable in which characters miss crucial clues of impending doom because they cannot or refuse to read the portents all around them. As in Zeami's and other Noh pieces, her structure is episodic, neither driven by suspense nor by psychological investigation. Each sequence illustrates a facet of the parable of indecisive, narcissistic, and corrupt rulers bringing about and orchestrating an ecological disaster.

Like Zeami, Cixous fashions a work in which the inanimate and the organic live and have a will seemingly independent of the characters: "My heart," says heroine Duan, "wants to leave this story" (p. 71). Spirit is everywhere and when ignored, as it is so often in Noh, places human life in jeopardy. Such ignorance means that characters perform acts of compartmentalization and opposition (such as pitting the City against the Country or Art against Commerce) that lead inevitably to destruction. The mighty cannot hear, for example, the framing dream which announces the catastrophe.

Cixous explains that the play is about the breakdown of the social "immune system" and about how this system begins to destroy itself through the emergence of the possibility of evil (Prenowitz 2004: 11). Characters succumb to evil because they fail to see the enemy within themselves, because they have lost touch with the interconnectedness of their universe, and because they have destroyed the necessary balance between aspects of the world one might differentiate as "natural," "man-made," and "spiritual." In Cixous' play, all is living; and everything living is given on-stage shape. The River/The Water proves the most devastating because it is the least listened to. Mirror of the future, water is never just "water," but humans are too lazy to grasp the life in it and its potential for both supreme devastation and new beginnings.

In *Drums on the Dam*, Cixous shows us a medieval and imaginary Chinese monarch, Lord Khang, who has ceded his forests and his moral compass to his rapacious nephew, Hun. In destroying the forest, Hun has laid the land open to massive flooding, flooding which turns into total havoc because the dams in place cannot hold, as in their construction they, too, have been subject to the cheating and dishonesty of their builders. In this malicious and egotistical world, a few characters have the vision or find the courage to attempt to save the populations at risk from the breaches in the dams. The Soothsayer and his daughter Duan, in particular – the latter transforming herself into a fervent warrior and leader of the sentinels guarding the countryside – try to prevent disaster from happening. The peasant sentinels, flood drummers sutured to their drums on top of the biggest dam, also offer an asylum of goodness, friendship, and safety. In contrast to the power structure, they keep watch over life, becoming a utopian destination, a potent haven for the "little people" – notably for the resolute noodle vendor, Mme Li, and her helper, Kisa, who were turned away from the closed doors of the City. All will nonetheless be swept away in the brutality and killing that accompany the flood. In the end, only Bai-Ju, the highly metaphorical puppet master, is left to fish out his puppets (smaller versions of the play's puppet characters) from the waters that invade and submerge the playing space. Forlorn, the puppets saved on the lip of the stage stare out at the audience at the production's close.

This last pantomime suggests many possible interpretations of the interaction between theater and life. One might be that, as in a baroque aesthetic, theater represents a world always becoming and always ending at the same time – unable to change its own course, fated to be what it is (a representation of itself), a world in which the striving for solidarity of a Duan can signal a new path but not guarantee its creation, a world in which the play for power, as in *Richard II*, inevitably ends in the end of power, a world in which, as Cixous puts it, "Power thinks it rules, yet it is ruled. And it is ruled over by death" (Prenowitz 2004: 11). Another interpretation would imply that only theater (or art) is saved by the kind of flood or purification vested on Lord Khang's empire. Theater, then, can see, but a seeing theater does not necessarily mean a visionary world. Human beings can become unthinking "puppets" if they stop paying attention, if their eyes do not, in fact, see. Given this thickness of meaning, the final scene interpolates the public, asking it: Can we act at all? Are we only acted upon? Or is life but a matter of modulation and struggle? In our puppet-like fragility, is there also a kind of puppet-like eternal "being there?" Finally, are we not doubled "puppets": a condensation and embodiment of something greater than ourselves but also only mere shells?

MNOUCHKINE'S BUNRAKU VISION

Mnouchkine's ongoing fascination with marionette forms led her to see the entire piece almost from the start as a puppet play, again paying homage to Asian arts. Bunraku, the near life-size Japanese puppet theater, provided her model; and as rehearsals developed with various actors trying out various roles – as is her practice – each one attempting to find a puppet form, it slowly emerged that some should also play the manipulators (or *koken*), the back-hooded puppeteers who had already influenced the look of the stage hands in *Richard II*. This development put a new spin on Mnouchkine's rehearsal practice of twinning, in which less experienced actors double master actors in the creation of a role. For in *Drums on the Dam*, the *koken* had to follow the movements being sketched out by the actor/puppets in order to fit themselves onto the stage and into the performance arc. At variance with bunraku practice, the actor/puppets were to speak their own lines, whereas in bunraku, narrators sit on stage and recite.

The most crucial variance was, of course, the fact that actual human actors played puppets. Mnouchkine's puppets were, thus, illusions of puppets (see Figure 3.6). In this sense, the Soleil *koken* were both closer and farther away from their Japanese models; human, as well, they had to perform "control" when they were, in fact, more of an appendage or secretion of the human puppet than its master. They were indeed integrated into rehearsals at the point where the actor/puppets felt themselves too heavy to continue to work alone.

In her contortion of traditional puppetry, Mnouchkine did observe the ritual of creating layers of death and resurrection, true of all great puppet theater. At ends of scenes and exits, for example, puppet bodies went limp and *koken* whisked them backwards offstage over the two upstage bridges. At such points, identifying structures encouraged the public's unsettling acceptance of "real" puppets and "real" puppeteers, the *koken* no longer seeming like doubled wraiths of the actor/puppets.

Mnouchkine's interest in actors as puppets and in the possibilities of the potent scenic alchemy of inorganic matter becoming organic through staged performance had been apparent long before *Drums on the Dam*. Starting with the key **mise-en-abime** scene at the end of *1789*, in which human guignol puppets represent the equally wooden-headed bourgeoisie's vision of the Revolution, she has created many sketches and vignettes with actors performing as puppets. To name another instance, in her 1989 collaboration with Hélène Cixous, *La Nuit miraculeuse*, a film for television, she had the "wax" statuary of Deputies to the Revolutionary Assembly come alive with the jerky, disarticulated movements later prominent in *Drums on the Dam*. This animation intimates how wonder emerges when stasis makes way for movement, cadence, and

Figure 3.6 The Lord Khang/puppet attends to his sly nephew Hun/puppet, as other puppets and their puppeteers look on, *Drums on the Dam*, 1999

rhythm in theater and also in the fundamental human choice to act, to build, or to advance the human community. With others, Mnouchkine has seen in the marionette the sublime extension of the actor's art: In marionette work, aesthetic control is all powerful, mastery of form dominates, and form – balance, lightness, gravity, line, rhythm – communicates the message and the emotion. Vanity, self-consciousness, and fear vanish.

STAGED HUMAN PUPPETRY

To set the stage for her illusory puppetry, Mnouchkine, as for *l'Indiade*, had her actors prepare by offering them a loosely organized study trip to Asia (Korea, Vietnam, Taiwan, Japan) before rehearsals began. Actors knew only that they would be working on a basic story of avarice and ecological disaster and that they should pay attention to puppet theater. Many ended their trip in Korea visiting Han Joe Sok, a master drummer who had earlier come to the Cartoucherie's ARTA to give a workshop: His son was later enlisted to train the puppet/sentinels in drumming for the flood-warning scene. From this initial trip, they gathered much of the iconic information that would help them develop their puppet/ characters. During the six months of rehearsals, actors endeavoring to find their puppet form helped, through improvisation, shorten and rewrite Cixous' text, seeking a more concise language appropriate to puppet expression. Mnouchkine slowed down their movement and set the gestures and stage pictures.

Actors created rehearsal costumes as they worked along, taking their inspiration from a combination of Asian theatrical forms. These were eventually fixed and sewn by the Soleil's costume team in Mnouchkine's usual palette of red, black, and gold. Actors also imagined their own masks out of stockings – later perfected and improved by Erhard Stiefel – to flatten and distort their features and give them an impassive countenance. They wore half gloves to help them keep fingers flat and bound together in order to achieve the unarticulated look of puppet hands. They slowly developed other-worldly speaking voices, using a staccato rhythm and somewhat nasalized pitch. They learned to deliver their lines posed and frontally, "held up" by the puppeteers, who also often manipulated the recurrent hand props: fans, parasols, swords, lanterns for night scenes, and a noodle cart.

In the production, stage pictures – as always well-balanced, almost sculpted – were set against twenty-two cascading silk backdrops, almost all evoking, in blue-gray pastels, landscapes and skyscapes. The backdrops gently located the place of action, while the black-clad *koken* helped indicate a time frame, fading in and out of vision, depending on the intensity of the lighting and the hue of the backdrops. The overriding sense was of a timeless watery dreamscape, with stage action happening in a temporary "safety zone," a metaphorical dam breached at the play's end by the always threatening water. (The filmed version of *Drums on the Dam* (2000) figures this flooding by immense sheets of billowing blue silk, as Mnouchkine felt that the visual impact of the onstage flood waters would not be the same on film as in live theater.)

With Jean-Jacques Lemêtre, Mnouchkine also established a multifaceted musical accompaniment. Positioned stage right, Lemêtre created a constant musical underscoring using mainly Asian string, wind, and drone instruments. He also interjected an eerie vocalization. His instrumentation (minor chords and discordant sawing) also commented on the action, dialogued occasionally with the characters, and gave rhythm to their gesturing, underlining the puppets' glide-walk during stage crossings. So as to always seem "animated," the actor/puppets were never completely still, shifting hands and heads to help maintain a feeling of puppets searching for equilibrium.

The most stunning moments of the production involved the combat and killing scenes with actor/puppets held aloft leaping and plunging, or rather, made to seem as if manipulated to leap and plunge. In these moments of prodigious physical action, the crucial ensemble work was undeniable. A form of non-individuated choral body emerged. "Blood" (strings of red yarn) circulated from the actor/puppets' wounds to the actor/puppeteers' hands, joining them in unquestionable communion. This mutual reliance echoed in form and function the meaning of the flood drummers, the collective hero of the production. The latter – connected morally to the exposed populations – were also connected to each other and to their overhead puppeteers (in an ingenious variation of string puppets) by an elaborate system of pulleys (see Figure 3.7).

THE PLACE OF *DRUMS ON THE DAM*

Drums on the Dam can be considered part of an important international theatrical movement which is rethinking puppetry and performance,

Figure 3.7 The sentinels/puppets keeping watch over the countryside practice their drum warnings, led by Duan, the Soothsayer's daughter, *Drums on the Dam*, 1999

indeed rethinking, since the 1960s, the boundaries of theater – between not only theater and puppetry but also between theater and dance and theater and sculptural form. This has led to experiments in size, as with the giant mobile shapes of the French company, Le Royal Deluxe, and to projections of the psyches of characters as forms accompanying their differently composed exterior selves, as in Dario Fo's staging of the opera, *The Italian Girl in Algiers* (1994), or as in all of **Tadeusz Kantor**'s work. Companies use all types of puppetry, as does the remarkable Handspring Puppet Company of South Africa, to foreground the difference between ideals and reality, to comment on and chastise contemporary demons of exoticism, racism, and exploitation. Modern puppetry extends the reach of actors by prosthetics, as in the case of Julie Taymor's *The Lion King* (1997). Such rethinking of theatrical boundaries has also meant reconceptualizing the actor as puppet or puppet-like (as in most of the work of Robert Wilson) or theorizing the single actor as both puppet and puppeteer (as in the theory of **Brecht**). This theoretical movement refuses to limit puppetry to children's art or to *kitsch* cabaret. We are, rather, in a realm of abstract symbolism, where the visual possibilities of animated objects onstage can be exploited in myriad ways – as, for example, in the expressionistic sculpted figures of brain-dead humans in Kantor's *The Dead Class* (1977).

In the above examples, the puppeteer is not invisible, nor meant to be "unseen" as is the convention of bunraku. Rather, the puppeteer is part and parcel of the art of representation. This dual presence of puppet and puppeteer allows for a sophisticated probing of the nature of theater – placing onstage the inseparable connection between the work of art and the artist. Giving form to the work of creation, the new puppet theater, Mnouchkine's work included, draws the audience into the richly suggestive space between animate and inanimate, where what is alive for sure is the act of theater itself.

CONCLUSION

Despite the differences we have seen in the four productions analyzed here, we can confidently point to certain commonalities true of all of Ariane Mnouchkine's productions. First and foremost is Mnouchkine's dedication to the "fanatically theatrical": "Neither journalism, nor television, nor cinema, [theatre] is not mere literature either. Theatre must remember that it is theatre [and thus must be] fanatically theatrical"

(Lecoq 1987: 130). All of Mnouchkine's work strives to create this alternative theatrical world which by its intense focus on form, on images, on bodies – even when texts are densely written, as with Cixous – makes spectators see what they ordinarily forget, or do not allow themselves to see. Her semiotically charged productions physically and sensually grab the public, putting it in touch with good and evil as though real forces in a melodramatic universe. Ironic detachment is not an option. Staged volumes, the rush of colors and textures, and music expand the contact and are integral to creating the mood and organizing the message.

Every Mnouchkine production also bears witness to the past and to the most brutal lessons of political history: how power corrupts, how extremes of identity and compartmentalization lead to strife, even to genocide and civil war. Every production also speaks to the future: from projections of utopia positing love as a possibility to projections of apocalypse where hate must win. Her 2003 turn in *Le Dernier Caravansérail* to the contemporary situation of Central Asian refugees denotes a willingness to move from dreams and visitations of the past to poetic forms that interrogate the here and now. The characters in *Le Dernier Caravansérail*, recalling the hyper-real aesthetic developed in *l'Indiade*, urge us to look at the present directly in the face, absorbing the ghastly and tragically predictable grotesqueness of current geopolitics.

4

PRACTICAL EXERCISES
Helen Richardson with Judith G. Miller

[Were I to give interviews about my life and work], I would feel that I were saying something definitive, when, on the contrary, I don't think of myself at all as a definitive being. In fact, I think one can never think of oneself as definitive and certainly not when one does theatre. For theatre is the art of absolute impermanency.

(Pascaud 2005: 7)

Theater's impermanency pervades Ariane Mnouchkine's practice, for her methods and techniques evolve with each new production. Each theater piece involves considerable research toward understanding the story and culture of the characters, and a long rehearsal process in search of the theatrical form for generating the idea of the show. Form is indeed the basis for the "theatricalization" she affects, determining how the text is communicated. Training and preparation center on the pursuit of theatricality, where the actor's body becomes an expressive instrument, not only of the personal states of the characters, but also of the characters' positions in society and their relationship to the community, both local and global. In this sense, we see a clear relationship with the practice of Jacques Lecoq.

Constant innovation means that each rehearsal process takes on a somewhat unpredictable life of its own. As former Soleil member and Co-director of ARTE Jean-François Dusigne describes it: "Each show has its own set of laws" (Personal Interview with Judith Miller, July 8, 2003). Such living quality is so important to Mnouchkine that it would be foolhardy to attempt to present specific exercises as unchanging to her rehearsal process. Indeed, each production starts with its own exercise protocol. Mnouchkine will, for example, invite guest artists to offer a particular set of exercises to nourish a particular production, that is, a **kathakali** expert may come in and teach dances and mudras (specific hand gestures) as for *The House of Atreus Cycle*, or an actor from another troupe (such as **Peter Brook**'s Sotigui Kouyaté) may be asked to provide exercises that stimulate collaboration.

Nevertheless, from show to show a certain spirit of work emerges, an attitude that evokes both complete devotion to the craft of theater and commitment to the idea of a collective – that is, the creation of a performing body in which every member of the Théâtre du Soleil is a part. Actors, in fact, move in and out of administrative or technical work with each production according to how successful they are in rehearsal in realizing the project's formal ideal. Mnouchkine herself bodies forth this spirit and communicates it to all who work with her, either in the free workshops which regularly precede the launching of a new piece – and from where several of the new actors for the production will come – or in the rehearsals themselves.

In this chapter, we will try to capture that spirit, and with it convey Ariane Mnouchkine's ethics of theater work. Through the ruminations of director and teacher Helen Richardson, who spent eight months in all with the Théâtre du Soleil (1987–91), participating in and transcribing two workshops and following rehearsals for *l'Indiade* and *The House of Atreus Cycle*, and through her long experiences as a director of university students using techniques inspired by working with Ariane Mnouchkine, we will explore how, in light of Mnouchkine's practice, one might apply her principles of theatrical engagement. We will also examine how to conduct a mask workshop – mask working being fundamental to her research. This extrapolation of basic principles will also reveal a rehearsal vocabulary (appended at the end of this chapter) that relates to the creative process as practiced at the Théâtre du Soleil, and that might serve those who would hope to pursue theater work in the spirit of the company. We believe that those who have participated or do participate in the collective adventure that is the Théâtre du Soleil will recognize their theater community in what follows.

PRINCIPLES OF THEATRICAL CREATION

When one explores something, one accepts the risk of getting lost.

(Féral 1998: 17)

Imagine that you are about to embark on a theatrical adventure that will take you into unknown territory, where the principles of theatrical creation are not always clear, where you will create a new piece with fellow theater-makers from around the globe that has never before been performed about a story that concerns people whose lives you are just beginning to know. You have no specific role, as yet, and what you achieve will be based on your ability to understand the continually evolving needs of the voyage, through the scope of your imagination and your commitment to your colleagues and the craft of theater. This sort of theatrical endeavor has been the path of Ariane Mnouchkine and her troupe for over the last forty years. In order to embark on such a journey there are some guiding principles that Mnouchkine has evolved over time. They start with the willingness to begin from zero, to acknowledge that each project has its own requirements, and that one must be ready to research and rediscover the basic rules of theatrical engagement for each new creation.

EMBARKING

Approaching theater-making without a clear destination and without a clear role can leave one full of trepidation. What if we lose our way and fall off the edge; what if we do not know enough about how to steer away from possible disasters? What if we find nothing?

There are certain basic strategies that can help further the possibility of arriving at a place of theatrical accomplishment and dynamic vision. These principles include

- a commitment to collaboration and community, which may include collective creation;
- the creation of a beautiful empty space and thus an atmosphere that engages the imagination;
- music that supports the body of the actor in his/her search for the passions and rhythms of the text;

- costumes that reveal the character;
- stage action which is metaphorical.

Working with masks provides Mnouchkine and the Théâtre du Soleil with a foundation for achieving theatricality. All of the above elements, in addition to masks, should be present from the beginning of the rehearsal process.

How to create a feeling of community, how to approach collaboration

> The [theatre] director has already achieved the greatest degree of power he has ever had in history. And our aim is to move beyond that situation by creating a form of theatre where it will be possible for everyone to collaborate without there being directors, technicians and so on, in the old sense.
>
> (Williams 1999: 1)

To begin a voyage into uncharted territory, you must first have a committed crew and an able leader. Community cannot be forced. It must, however, be recognized as the basis for all theatrical endeavor and it must be exercised through present mindedness. This means such basic rules of engagement as acknowledging your fellow travelers when you first meet them and at the beginning of each rehearsal. No matter what one's position, no one should be too busy to greet or too unimportant to be greeted. This acknowledgment establishes a sense of community and mutual respect.

Present mindedness requires that each member of the troupe, whatever their function – be it actor, director, designer, stage manager, playwright, or musician – be available and ready to partake in the general demands of theater, whether it is helping with administration, setbuilding, clean-up, or making lunch. This allows everyone to appreciate the work of others, and to experience ownership of the whole enterprise. Community is also about care of space and attentiveness to time. Everyone takes note of the space and makes sure to keep things in order and be on time.

Collaboration starts with listening to the other and learning to receive from the other. Leadership is about recognizing the abilities of others and helping them to realize those abilities. Rather than arriving at the rehearsal with a grand plan as to the direction of the production, the leader arrives ready to observe. With great acuity, she or he must watch the work of the creative team of actors, playwright, designers, and musicians in order to understand how a production can realize itself, with an eye to achieving a significant theatrical vision.

While the director might be the acknowledged overall leader of the enterprise, creative leadership can be exercised by an actor, the playwright, musician, or designer through a demonstration of inventiveness that leads the enterprise to greater accomplishment. Observing the process of rehearsal is not exclusively the domain of the director. In a collaborative venture, it is important that all members of the creative team observe the process in order to adjust and improve on designs, text, and staging as the rehearsals progress. The musicians especially are always present as, along with the actors, they are improvising the story and thus aiding the actors to realize their actions.

Actors who are not on the stage working on a scene should be sitting in the bleachers, watching with great attentiveness. In a collaborative effort, it is extremely important that every actor knows what the whole group is about: One actor's accomplishments will become the inspiration for another actor's invention. Actors also learn from each other through imitation, a form of godfathering and godmothering. This allows the actors to teach each other and learn from each other. There should be no assumption of ownership when it comes to creative ideas. There is always the possibility that another actor will take the idea presented to the next level and beyond.

A community includes all who are in some way or other involved with the production. If the creation touches on contemporary issues, then there will be the need to engage with those who are the subject of the piece. There should be meetings with them, interviews, visits to their communities, and environments. Ultimately, they should be invited to observe the work. If the work is historical, then the creative community can evolve through engaging with experts, doing extensive research, visiting landmarks, and reading first person accounts.

The sense of community should not be reserved only for those within the troupe but also for all the visitors and the audience. The audience might be invited to observe respectfully the actors as they prepare themselves for performance. This period of observation – which goes both ways, as actors greet friends in the audience, or acknowledge the attentive gaze of an audience member – engenders a feeling of communion that can transform the performance. During the performance, actors should maintain a direct relationship with the audience by facing them even as they speak to their fellow actors onstage. There should be no fourth wall. The characters will share their struggles not only with other characters onstage, but also with the audience before them.

EXERCISES

Toward an ensemble

There are many exercises that encourage community and collaboration. The following exercises from Sotigui Kouyaté of the Peter Brook Company, who has in the past given workshops at the Théâtre du Soleil, are very effective in fostering collaboration.

The clapping exercise

The clapping exercise is a simple and effective exercise, which encourages first efforts at opening up group communication and establishes a spirit of generosity and receptivity. It is important that it be done with care and precision.

- Make a circle.
- A leader within the circle gives his/her energy to the person on the right by sending a clap in the direction of their neighbor to the right. This is done by bringing the right hand to the left in a firm clap and letting the left hand slide off the right hand in the direction of the person on the right.
- The right hand must meet the left hand in a firm clap, while the left hand keeps on moving toward the direction of the neighbor on the right.
- The sound of the clap should be strong and clear.
- While the leader is sending his/her clap to the neighbor, he or she makes sure to establish eye contact with the neighbor.
- The neighbor receives the gesture of the clap through the eyes, and then turns to the neighbor at the right and passes on the gesture, also making eye contact with the neighbor to the right and keeping the same strong sound of the single clap.

- The passing of the single clap continues all the way around the circle accompanied by eye contact, with the same strong sound of the clap. A constant rhythm around the circle must be maintained.
- This sending of a clap continues around the circle for as long as it takes to establish strong claps, clear eye contact, and a consistent rhythm around the circle.
- Once everyone has mastered the exercise, the leader can begin to vary the exercise by sending a clap in the opposite direction, to the neighbor on the left.
- As the group continues to master the exercise, members of the group can take the initiative of changing the direction of the clap at any time. As the direction changes, it is imperative that the rhythm of the clap remain clear and consistent and that the sound of the clap remain strong.
- This is an exercise that almost immediately engenders laughter and a sense of play and spontaneous communication.

This exercise can have many variations, such as

- the group can break out of the circle and send the clap to each other throughout the space, requiring the group to watch for the direction of the clap within the space;

or

- the group can be divided up into smaller groups, numbered 1–4, or more;
- the groups go off on their own and create their own particular set of claps with a specific rhythm;
- the whole group reconvenes and each group shares their clapping rhythm consecutively;
- the group works together to make the series of claps into a seamless clapping piece.

Walking, stopping, and starting

This exercise is more complex and often takes time and patience to accomplish.

- Count off 10 people in a group.
- The group of 10 moves to the center of a circle made by the remaining participants.

- The group of 10 begins to walk at their own individual pace.
- When the group of 10 feels it is time, they stop walking, *one person at a time*.
- If more than one person stops at the same time, the group of 10 must start over; going back to walking until they accomplish stopping as a group, *one person at a time*.
- Once stopped, when the group of 10 feels it is time, they start to walk *one person at a time*. Again, if more than one person starts at the same time, the group of 10 must start over, all of the group coming to a stop and trying again to start *one person at a time*.
- Once the group has accomplished the above task, they must next stop and start two people at a time, then three, four, five, six, seven, eight, nine, and finally ten people.
- All stopping and starting must be done clearly and without hesitation.
- It is important to know when to take the initiative and when to cede to others the action of stopping or starting.
- The task of the outside circle is to observe and make sure that the rules of the exercise are followed.
- The object is to sense each other in the group.
- The exercise cannot be forced. Be calm and patient. Allow movement to happen when it needs to.
- Be careful not to get into a rhythm of starting or stopping.
- Do not signal each other.

Devising theater in the spirit of Mnouchkine

What happens to other people happens to us as well.

(Pascaud 2005: 151)

Although the Théâtre du Soleil can be a daunting role model for making theater, there is actually much to be gained by experimenting with its methods. Mnouchkine views her process as a constant return to school in order to delve into the roots of theater and its importance to the world community. By exploring theatrical forms and styles of acting, as well as seeking to understand ensemble work through improvisation and the collective process of play creation, Mnouchkine has contributed significantly to the revitalization of theater and to theater's claim to be a progressive forum for social change.

Collective creation is at the core of Mnouchkine's method. This includes the creation of text, character, staging, set, and costume. Even as regards the evolution of a character, various actors may work on a character in rehearsal, although only one of them might ultimately perform that role. Everyone in the company grows through observation and sharing.

It is true that the Théâtre du Soleil has a long rehearsal process, but interesting and well-made collective creations can be done in shorter rehearsal periods. Collective creation often results in an accelerated process due to the enormous motivation of an engaged ensemble.

THE BENEFITS OF COLLECTIVE CREATION

- Actors are more motivated when they are asked to be primary creators, therefore, growing more quickly in the work.
- Actors are more engaged; they tend to take greater risks and are willing to challenge themselves in new ways that result in more exciting theater from the inception of the rehearsal process.
- As the work comes out of the actors' skills and knowledge, their capacity to perform the work is more immediate.
- Ensemble creations have greater synergy, which translates as quicker problem solving, and a more dynamic and fluid approach to rehearsal and performance.
- Actors are more willing to work for the greater whole when they are in partnership with each other, the director, and playwright, and therefore they are willing to make decisions more quickly and efficiently, saving time in the process.

Mnouchkine-inspired tenets of devising collectively

- A theme should be introduced that is capable of exciting an ensemble of theater-makers.
- The leader should insist on research into the theme through readings – including historical, technical, and poetic narratives – watching films, looking at pictures, conducting interviews.
- The ensemble takes form through group exercises and the sharing of individual talents, research, and creation, as well as in smaller group endeavors.
- Exercises take the form of working with masks and other forms of physical communication and theatricalization, including choral

work, corporeal language through gesture, and work with music, itself developed in harmony with the evolution of the production.

- The text is created through individual and group efforts, after research and during improvisations. Staging often emerges at the same time as the text. It always includes addressing the audience directly and acknowledging the theatrical space.
- Costumes are developed from the first day of rehearsal as the actors transform themselves with whatever materials they have at their disposal. This stimulates the imagination and protects the process from the mundane and the conventional.
- Casting evolves organically through the commitment and the success of the various individual members of the ensemble as they try out roles.
- The process is respected and observed by all: actors, designers, and writers when they are not working on a specific problem. Everyone's energetic attention results in the consensus that fixes a scene or a moment.
- Before the performance begins, the audience is invited to observe the actors in their final stages of transformation. This experience emphasizes the theatricality of the experience for both the actors and the audience and also engages the audience deeply in the theatrical journey.

TOWARD A MAGNIFICENT EMPTY SPACE

The stage should be like a bare hand offering up the actors.

(Féral 1998: 32)

The theater work must evolve in a space that evokes universality, where everything is possible and where theatricality can emerge without the distraction of the day to day. Discovery is dependent on imagination, the ability to see what one could not see previously. You must focus on communal spaces, spaces where political power and social engagement are exercised. Just as in the theater of Aeschylus and Shakespeare, the emphasis should be on a metaphorical space that can represent many places, that can evoke the theme of the play, that will acknowledge the place of community as represented not only by the actors but by the audience as well.

How often do we walk into a rehearsal space or classroom that is filled with furniture and props that are being used by other groups working on different theater productions or exercises? In this cluttered space, we are expected to create a world specific to our own work. It is important to find a way to minimize the distractions within a space. How can one accomplish this in a world of shared spaces? If the room cannot be emptied, one can consider putting everything away as much as possible, and then draping neutral material over anything that is extraneous to the work, so that the actor's imagination can begin to breathe and to invent. A home can be signified by the rolling out of a carpet in an empty space, a town square by the rolling up of the carpet and the placement of the actors on the periphery of the space, delineated by walls that now serve as barricades. In another scene, the walls can be transformed, depending on how the actors engage with the environment. Versatility and poetic expression are as important in the creation of the space as in the movement of the actors. The particulars of a scenic space created by the actors, the music, set pieces, and props should represent, in a poetic sense, an aspect of the world order experienced in the play.

Exercises in creating space

Imaging place

- Start with an empty space.
- Imagine the circumstances of the play.
- Try to establish these circumstances through the action of the actors (the actors should be in costume) and through the use of music.
- Discover what is the minimal amount of set needed to convey the place of the play, perhaps a throne (a low table or a simple chair in the middle of an empty space to suggest a seat of power, or a rug to suggest a home).
- The actors should move though the different environments of the play, working on, for example, how a king walks through an empty palace or through a forest or through an assembly of the people or through a battlefield after victory and after defeat.
- Or the actors should explore how a young woman walks through a holy temple or through the door of her secret lover's house or through the town square late at night or to school through a busy street.
- Work on versatility. Take one piece of furniture, such as a table, and discover how many places it can represent through the way it can be used.

- The point of the exercise is to find out how the space can support and be supported and defined by the actor's imagination.

Entrances and exits

- In an empty space, begin by establishing the places of entrance and exit.
- The actors must, through their actions, establish the place as soon as they enter and maintain their relationship to this specific place until the moment they exit.
- The actors must know what particular place they are entering into. Is it a busy street, their home, their place of work, the home of a fellow conspirator, the foothills of the Himalayas at the start of winter? The actor establishes the location and makes it come alive through clear actions.

CREATING TEXTUAL AND PHYSICAL MUSICALITY

[We must] hear a spoken voice as a song.

(Féral 1998: 48)

There should be no rehearsal or creative work without music. Just as in Asian theater, the text must be accompanied by music. Music does not push the actor into emotional states, but allows the actor to enter into a world where the condition for these states exists. Music can help establish the rhythm of an action; it can set the scene by evoking the landscape, whether it is the sea, high mountains, a vast desert, a busy street, or a lonely outpost. It takes a great deal of collaborative work to find the proper tones and rhythms to support the action of the actors. The music has to complement the text rather than cancel it out. Depending on the actor's formation, some actors might ignore the music for a long time before they let it seep into their consciousness. It is important to devise exercises for the actors in which they must concentrate on listening, in which they learn to act in collaboration with the music, respond to changes in tone and rhythm, stop their actions to let the music resonate before continuing on. The music should transport everyone to a place where actions of great magnitude can take place. One should not be afraid to have music throughout the rehearsal to stimulate states of feeling, even if in performance one may not always have music. Orchestrating the piece is an important part of the work and should be done carefully. Such orchestration is indispensable in helping create the theatricality of the piece.

Not every one has a full time musician at their disposal, although this is often normal for dance classes. However, much can be done to assure that there is always an atmosphere of music to inspire the actors. Sometimes it is possible for actors in the ensemble, who are able to engage in musical collaboration, to provide musical accompaniment. Recorded music, carefully chosen to evoke the scenes or exercises being worked on, can be played as the actors work on their text.

Exercises can be devised as warm-ups in which the actors respond directly to the music before beginning text work. Often, as the actor begins working on the text, he/she seems to be oblivious to the music. Nonetheless, there is a subliminal support that can be seen in the actors' willingness to engage more quickly or more deeply in poetic action. The music says, "Come play with me," and eventually the actor almost always does.

Exercises in creating musicality

Live music is preferable. The musicians must support and enhance the work of the actors; they must be willing to enter into the actions and text of the characters.

Listening

- Play music that is connected to the world of the play.
- The actors move with the music and stop when the music stops. The starting and stopping should be clear and specific.
- Now, specify a phrase or specific section of rhythm in the music; the actors must stop every time they hear that phrase/section and start when the phrase/section is completed.

Speaking the text

- Actors take a part of their text and begin it at a certain point with the music.
- The actor notices when the music encourages a pause in the text and when it suggests that the text continue. (This exercise demands that each actor take a turn in executing the pauses and continuations.)

Moving to music

- Actors enter onstage with the music, showing the rhythm of the characters as they cross the stage and exit. This exercise is nonverbal and should involve a concrete action, which can be as simple as walking. This exercise must not be about dancing with the music. If the actor should dance, the dance should show a concrete action, such as a celebration or an act of mourning.

Improvising to music

- Play music that has dramatic variation. (Wagnerian and most nineteenth-century classical music is good for this exercise.)
- The actors are given a scene to play that is nonverbal. Each actor is told his or her action in confidence. (Example: scene – two young women, room-mates, are sleeping; they wake up. Actor one suspects actor two of having a secret affair with her lover; she wants to confront her but is afraid that her suspicions are wrong and she will ruin their friendship. On the other hand, if it is true, she may find herself reacting violently. Actor two is supremely happy; she has just met the love of her life, but she has promised her lover that she will keep their relationship a secret.)
- The object of the exercise is for the actors to use the music to further the action and to support their emotional states. This means that the music will dictate the evolution of the improvisation. Actors must use the music to support their actions and not fight or ignore it.
- The actors may need to be side-coached to remember to listen to the music at various points in the exercise.
- Again, the point is not to dance with the music, but to find the action within the music.

CREATING A SECOND SKIN

> The costume is the actor's second skin, and the only skin of the character. Getting costumed is re-finding one's childhood: joy, disguise, processionals, and metamorphoses. It's thanks to costumes that actors become other.
>
> (Féral 1998: 33)

There should be no rehearsal without costumes. From day one the actors must be in the process of transforming themselves. The leader of the group might suggest a possible starting point, colors, and looks that relate to the play. The designers might provide costume material and the actors should experiment and improvise with the material. Together, working as an ensemble, the designers, actors, and director will eventually discover the appropriate costumes for the production.

The costumes should resonate with each other and suggest they come from within the same world. They should be able to transcend the quotidian and become signs of universal qualities, while at the same time suggesting the particularities of a character. There should be mirrors available for the actors to observe themselves as they create the appearance of their characters. The costume area should be organized and tidy, so that it does not impede on the stage, but is quickly accessible if an actor wants to try a different costume. There should be a place for the actors to store their street clothes and other items that are not specific to the rehearsal, so that they are out of the way of the area of creation. The costume designer should be available, regularly, to observe rehearsals and suggest how the costumes could be enhanced.

Few productions, or classes doing scene work, have the costume resources of the Théâtre du Soleil. However, it is important for actors to begin rehearsal by discarding their own street clothes and creating that second skin, which will eventually evolve into the characters. With every successive rehearsal, as the actors put on their costumes, they transform into their characters more easily and more deeply.

At the first day of rehearsal, temporary costumes can be provided that inspire the creation of the characters and the world of the play. If stock is available, the costumes can be pulled from the stock; if not, the actors can collaborate on bringing together basic rehearsal costumes. There should be the possibility of some flexibility within the costumes; various choices for hats, scarves, shoes, jackets, shirts, pants, dresses, or skirts. The costumes should avoid evoking a specific period, and, especially, avoid suggesting a realistic approach that discourages theatrical choices on the part of the actors. Rather, the costumes should suggest certain general qualities or social positions, such as wealth, power, status, or poverty – or businessman, servant, lover, seductress, scholar, etc.

Exercises in creating a second skin

These exercises should encourage the actors to transform into their characters, observe the line and shape of their characters, and discover the movements and gestures of the characters as suggested by the costume. Actors, like painters, create the image of their characters in collaboration with the costume designer, director, and fellow actors. The following exercises should be done with great care.

Disguising oneself

- Provide a variety of costumes that support the characters and the world of the play.
- The actors should study their characters in the mirror as they transform themselves, taking the time to add hats or gloves, or scarves in order to complete the disguise.
- The actors' goal should be to disguise themselves so that a clear transformation is established.
- The disguise must be completed: is there a part of the actor's appearance that interrupts the lines of the character; are there aspects of the costume that are incomplete or careless? There should be nothing left untouched, unchanged.

Discovering the character

- The actor in costume stands before the mirror and contemplates the character.
- What does the character have to say? The actor begins by listening.
- The actor moves with the character, studying the character's gestures and movements.
- Does the gesture follow the line of the character or is it imposed? Do the movements reveal the character or do they muddy the character?

First steps

- The actor is given an action, such as entering the town square to meet up with a lover or to find a missing child in a crowded street or to steal food from an outdoor vendor.
- The actor makes an entrance onto the stage, establishing his or her character immediately through movement and gestures that complete the lines of the character.
- The actor continues across the stage completing the action and then exiting.

- Feedback is given to help the actor specify more concretely the appearance of the character. It is important not to encourage posing, but to find the character through specific actions. The other actors participating in the exercise should observe and learn about their own characters through observing other characters.
- The actor must move in such a way as to share the character with the audience rather than to obscure the character.

TOWARD ACTION AS METAPHOR

> The genius of the West is in the texts and the genius of the East is in the actor's work, in the form.
>
> (Féral 1998: 39)

The actor's process should be a constant search for theatricality, for a metaphorical and poetic expression of experience. How can one encourage the actor to find a physical expression of the poetry of the text? How can one get past the tendency to express ideas in day to day gestures, which lack imagination and creativity? How can the actor be encouraged to discover metaphorical actions? In order to create a space that allows for imaginative action, the leader must show the actors pictures that inspire the imagination, or set the scene through describing a situation poetically, as if telling a story: "Once upon a time, there was a village high in the mountains. A caravan stopped by one last time before the snow came . . . ."

Exercises to provoke metaphorical actions

A picture is worth . . .

- Bring pictures from magazines or newspapers, postcards or prints of paintings, etc., which show people doing concrete actions that suggest various levels of meaning.
- Recreate the image in the picture with the actor's body. Ask what the movement and gestures say. Ask how many meanings are behind the image.
- Change the quality of the gestures. Discuss how the meaning changes.

Snapshots

- A group of actors stands in a circle. Three to five members of the circle go into the center.
- One of the circle group takes a drum and beats it vigorously while the actors in the center move about within the circle, moving up and down and around, making strong choices in movement.
- The actors stop when the drum stops and freeze into position, no matter how awkward the position.
- The actors on the outside of the circle must quickly come up with a title for the image formed by the frozen actors.
- Once the title is decided on, the circle of actors can adjust the frozen actors, ever so slightly, to further shape the image to the title. Then the frozen actors can return to the circle.
- This exercise should be repeated, encouraging actors to find titles as quickly as possible, strengthening the "readability" of the image.

Storytelling through images

- The same exercise as above is repeated three times with the same actors in the center. Three different images and titles are established.
- The actors within the circle recreate once again the three different images in their original sequence.
- The outside circle of actors creates a narrative using the three images, in whatever order they wish, which become the beginning, middle and end of a story. A new title is created for the whole sequence of images.

Once upon a time – telling the plot of the play as if it were a story

- The actors sit in a circle and take turns telling the story of the play they are working on by starting with "Once upon a time . . . ."
- It is important that as the actors tell the story they be very specific about the atmosphere and setting, so that everyone is transported to the place, time, and mood of the play: "there was a village nestled between two high mountain peaks where the air was heavy with the smell of dying blossoms . . . ."
- The actors should be equally specific when describing the appearance of the characters, their gestures, and actions.

MASK WORK

> I think that the mask doesn't hide the actor but rather the self. In fact, the mask hides nothing at all, but rather reveals. It's a magnifying glass for the soul, a peep hole in which to see the soul. With the mask, all theatrical laws fall into place.
>
> (Féral 1998: 29)

HOW THE MASK ASSURES THEATRICALITY

The work of the actor should begin with the mask. Working with a mask is the first step toward discovering theatricality. The mask, like a divine object, catalyzes the actor's transformation. It allows the actor to forget the self and to incarnate the other. Through observing the mask and letting it live through the body, the actor is able to enter into a character without psychologyzing the other or needing to identify with the inner psyche of the other. Working with masks is not about learning characters' subconscious desires, or subtext, but about understanding their place in society, their relationship to the world around them. The mask imposes an acute form that requires the actor to complete it, not in a single manner, but in a multitude of ways. The mask is a severe master that reveals all errors in action and forces the actor to focus on details.

It is important that the mask be of a certain quality. Masks that are poorly crafted or generic will deaden the work of the actor rather than catalyze it. Masks should animate actors and not rigidify them. The mask should evoke human experience rather than hiding or distorting it. Bizarre or distorted masks, which deny the beauty in a character, should be avoided.

It takes effort to find or create good masks. Workable quality **Balinese masks** can sometimes be found in Asian import stores at a reasonable cost. Research can be done to find quality mask-makers. There are several organizations that sell masks over the Internet, but beware of the decorative mask, which is of no use in theater work. You can also fashion your own masks through working with plaster-based materials, or through making papier-mâché masks; a naive, home-made mask will work better than a highly decorated mask that is intended for display rather than for work on the stage.

To see if a mask is suited for theater work, put it on and observe it in the mirror. If it surprises you by allowing you to see the world in a new way, inspiring specific actions and evoking particular character traits, then it is likely to be theatrically viable. If, on the other hand, you find yourself responding to the mask with dance-like or ambiguous movements, the mask is probably better left hanging on a wall.

A BASIC MASK WORKSHOP

Every so often Ariane Mnouchkine holds a public workshop on mask work as part of her company's service to the theater community and also in order to find new talent for the company. These workshops attract many theater-makers from across the globe, and only a fraction of the number who apply to the workshop can be accommodated (around 200 participants from an applicant pool of up to 1,200). These workshops give the participants an opportunity to experience the working process of the Théâtre du Soleil and can run anywhere from a week to a month. In what follows, we suggest the basic outlines for a mask workshop that would resonate with what Ariane Mnouchkine attempts to achieve in her own workshops.

Day 1: the rules of the work

On the first day of the workshop the leader must introduce the group to the ground rules.

1   Respect for the process and for all fellow travelers:

- The actor is on time.
- The actor is prepared.
- The actors assist their fellow actors in realizing the best performance possible. This means that the actors take turns working at different roles in rehearsal and, in principle, the actor who has best realized the role, by consensus of the ensemble, will play the role in performance.
- During the rehearsal, the actors not onstage watch, with close attention, the rehearsal process in order to learn from the struggles and achievements of their fellow actors.
- The training focuses on the "pleasure of playing." Improvisation is a fundamental part of this playing. In order to improvise, actors must know who their characters are, where they are, and what they want.

2   Respect for the space, and care of the space:

- The actor takes initiative to keep the space in order. The rehearsal begins with a swept, prepared stage, and ends with a clean stage.
- There are no street shoes in rehearsal. Only shoes reserved for the rehearsal floor are to be worn in the rehearsal space. Street shoes are left in a place reserved for them outside the rehearsal space.
- No eating, cell phones, etc., or extraneous items are allowed in the theater space.

3   Respect for the craft and the care that the craft demands:

- The actors begin the rehearsal by getting into costume for the characters they are to work on that day. No street clothes are allowed during rehearsal; the actor must transform himself or herself externally, as well as internally to realize a character. Materials will be provided for the actor to use in rehearsal. As creative members of the ensemble, actors will help shape their own costumes in collaboration with the ensemble. This ensemble includes the costume designer, who is present from day one of the rehearsal.
- Actors remain in costume until the end of the rehearsal, always ready to go onstage, even if it turns out they will not get to work onstage that day.
- Full attention to the work is expected.

A first improvisation

With the ground rules in mind, a first improvisation can be suggested. The leader should start with two volunteers, giving them their actions confidentially, and then putting on some emotionally evocative music, such as Mars' music from Horst's *Symphony of the Planets*. The exercise should be about playing one's actions while working with the music. After the exercise is over, the actors should critique themselves and be critiqued.

To achieve a successful improvisation, you must keep the following in mind:

- Being in the moment is the most fundamental requirement of the actor.

- Actors do not speak words but show emotions. The theater is emotion put into action. Words are emotions put into action.
- Find the "the interior music" of each character: not the noise, the music. Each character has his or her own rhythm and leitmotif, which should be apparent from the moment the actor enters the scene.
- Find in the other's look the strength to play. Dare to have the generosity to receive. Be concave in order to take in, and convex in order to project.
- Reject all stereotypical, learned, conventional approaches to character, and all pretensions.
- Look within the small precise moments to find the great moments.

Improvising in groups (the beginnings of collective collaboration)

Suggest a potentially rich improvisation, for example, an afternoon at the ice skating rink (to the music of Beethoven) or the interactions of a group of disparate people at a bus stop (to the music of Satie). The scenario should lend itself to many extravagant possibilities of movement, as well as to a variety of characters, for example, the novice skater, the show-off, the skater on the make, and the skater in pursuit, the skater whose skating is a threat to every living creature and the skater who lives in fear of every step he takes. It should also lead to a rich canvas of physical possibilities: shuffling, flinging oneself about, and gliding across the stage. At the end of the improvisation, take the time to discuss the emerging characters:

- How do the characters see the world; how do they respond to it? Does every movement of a specific character reflect the nature of the character?
- Does each actor avoid imposing him/herself in a scene without regard to the other characters, the atmosphere, or the obstacles that arise? Has each actor found his or her role, the role of the character, within the greater whole?

The object is to reach a state of passionate engagement in the situation, with each character's interior music humming away as all respond meticulously and spontaneously to the actions erupting around them. There should be no illustrations and no self-consciousness.

Day 2: meeting the masks

On this day, the actors meet the masks. The masks should be compelling and well crafted, perhaps in the tradition of Italian **commedia dell'arte**, with several versions of Arlecchino (the servant), Pantalone (the merchant), Matamore (the captain), Pulchinella (the peasant), and el Dottore (the doctor). More vividly colored wooden masks from the Balinese *commedia* tradition can also be used, for example, the old minister to the king with bushy white eyebrows, sideburns and a full mustache, the servant with large protruding teeth, the young peasant with wild eyes, or another young city man with a long gaunt face, large nose, and drooping eyes. The masks must exude strong characters.

Encountering the masks

Mask work is challenging and your first encounters with it can be daunting. The mask may feel uncomfortable and unnatural. The better the craftsmanship of the mask, the more comfortable the mask will tend to be. However, if the mask is painful to wear, foam can be glued on the inside of the mask in order to cushion the contact of the mask with the face. The cushioning should not be so thick as to push the mask off the face to the point where one cannot see the actors' eyes through the eyeholes of the mask. It is essential that the eyes of the actor be clearly visible through the eyeholes of the mask.

The eyeholes of the mask may seem to radically obscure your vision. When wearing the mask, it takes time to get used to the limitations on peripheral vision. However, over time, the body of the actor will develop new ways of seeing, and the actor's body will begin to sense the space around him or her more acutely.

Guidelines for how to make friends with the mask

- Be patient. First observe the mask off the face and then put it on.
- Take time in front of the mirror to get to know the mask.
- Make sure the mask is well placed on the face so that the eyes match up with the eyeholes, allowing you to see and allowing the spectator to observe the eyes behind the mask.
- Make sure the mask is secure so that it is not moving around on the face. It is best to put the strap of the mask up toward the back of

the crown of the head, as putting the strap toward the base of the head usually causes the mask to slip down.

- Let the mask observe its environment; do not feel the need to perform but rather allow yourself to respond.
- Let the mask find a task and then see how the mask does the task.
- Sometimes the work with the mask is a slow process; other times the possession is immediate and you will be whisked away into action. You need to be receptive to both experiences.
- Try to learn to love the mask; it is more likely to respond in kind.

Mnouchkine-inspired tenets of working with masks

1   Respect the mask. As Mnouchkine often says, "With the mask it is you who must yield. Seek a humble and loving encounter with your character. Fear of the mask is a wholesome fear such as one might feel when a god descends."

- The mask must be handled with care. Always hold it on the sides of the face, never on the nose or through the eyes. Never put the mask down on its face,

2   Observe the masks: Let the masks speak to you.

- Who are they?
- Where do they come from?
- What do they want?
- How do they get what they want?
- How does their body move and respond?
- What is their emotional state?
- What is their rhythm?

3   Find the costume for your mask.

- Make sure the mask, not the actor, is the focus. At best, the actor should be unrecognizable beneath mask and costume.
- When working with masks, your skin and hair should be hidden by gloves, long sleeves, turbans, scarves, leggings, and shoes to avoid mixing realism with theatricality.
- Look in the mirror to see if you have found the character.

4   Embody the mask.

- In creating your character, remember that you are already wearing the mask that defines the character's lines. It is your task to complete those lines through the body. If you try to impose movement on the character or ignore its nature, you will be faced with the tyranny of the mask that tolerates no false gestures or movements. However, if you allow yourself to submit to the requirements of the mask, the results can be magical.
- A good mask, although it may come out of a tradition, is protean. The mask may be that of an old man and embody very specific characteristics, such as large frown lines and a very long nose, but one cannot say that Pantalone, the old miser, can only be played one way. There are as many Pantalones and Arlecchinos as there are actors to embody them.

5   Share the mask

- The mask is presentational in form and demands frontality. The more you keep the mask toward the audience, the more effective the mask becomes.
- Let your character form a rapport with the audience; let it get the audience on its side.
- Do not forget that the mask exists only in direct relationship to the audience; the mask represents the magic of our confrontation with the archetypes that reside in the collective unconscious.
- In mask work we are seeing the basic states and characteristics of mankind presented in their rawest and most potent form.

The mask in action

A small group of costumes should be placed on the stage for the first step in the mask work.

- The leader asks for volunteers to go up and choose a mask that speaks to them, and costume themselves.
- The process of preparing should be done in complete silence. The act of transformation should be demanding and thorough. Those workshop participants who have done a good job of costuming

become unrecognizable, subsumed by their characters, embracing, not suffering, the transformation.

• More experienced actors may be asked to help the novice mask performers when they need assistance with, for example, their turbans or in developing a more complete and effective disguise.

The leader bids the masked performers to sit on the stage when they are done. She or he asks them simple questions about who they are, their name, their work, their family situation. The leader then requests that they come up onstage one at a time. A performer walks onstage. The interview continues, revealing the character by the way the character responds to the questions; for example, expressing anxiety, eagerness, or pride. At the end of the day, all characters should be established and the entire group should form itself into small troupes of around six members in preparation for the next day when the participants will work with masks in group improvisations.

Day 3: group improvisations (focus on the resistance)

The object is to help the workshop participants discover the theatricality inherent in the story of political resistance, a theme often at the forefront of Ariane Mnouchkine's work. The workshop participants' task is to work on the theme of resistance against a power that has invaded their country. The separate troupes will be working with the masks, although it will also be possible to have unmasked characters, such as in *commedia dell'arte* where the young *ingénu* characters, both male and female, are played by unmasked performers – their youthful beauty constituting their mask.

The process requires the troupes to develop loose scenarios and then determine which characters each member of the troupe will play. The troupes disperse across the bleachers. They should be encouraged to discuss possible story lines. The clearer the actions of the scenario and the characters, the more capable the actors will be in improvising a scene. The time for discussion comes to a close and everyone moves over to the costume area. There, each participant gathers together his or her costume and puts it on. When ready, everyone returns to sit on the bleachers with their troupe.

A first troupe is chosen and the actors must walk over to where the masks are displayed to choose their masks. Next, they move over to the mirrors to study themselves in their masks for several minutes, and then ascend to the stage, standing at the side to make their entrance. The entrance is the crucial moment and if it is not theatrical the group should be asked to sit down and another group should be called.

The actors will need to be reminded

- to become like children when creating theater: "Children love the act of playing. The presence of the masks keeps us from forgetting to play";
- that from the moment the character enters, the story begins. The actor must ask what the mask's emotional state is before entering the stage;
- that the actor must experience and exteriorize the interior music of the character. This music arises through the rhythm of the character's movements, as well as through the lines of the body;
- that once one enters the stage, one enters another continent, beginning a voyage where day to day language, vulgarity, and the prosaic cannot be used.

A good improvisation can last as long as 20 minutes. Each character should have his or her own distinct rhythm and own way of coping with the dangers of the invading army. At the same time, the actors should create a distinct community with clear relationships. At every moment, the actors must share their story with the audience through keeping the masks frontal, communicating with the entire community, while still maintaining communication with their fellow actors. The scene should work on a metaphorical level as well. The way the characters treat each other during this difficult journey might reveal the importance of respect and loyalty as a basis for survival of the group. At the same time, the group's highly formal structure might suggest the limitations of the social order and why the characters may need to escape an invading army. Through careful work with the masks and the imagination, the groups of actors should also be able to take the other workshop participants on their journey.

AN EXAMPLE OF TWO SUCCESSFUL IMPROVISATIONS (FROM A MNOUCHKINE WORKSHOP IN 1990 AT THE CARTOUCHERIE DE VINCENNES)

Resistance and a love story

Two soldiers enter in Balinese masks, the actors miming holding rifles as they walk by. As soon as the soldiers exit, two other characters (resistance members) come in very carefully and with great anxiety, their gestures suggesting that they are carrying a bomb. They set up a fuse and through one character's disdainful imitation of the statue that is in the center of the piazza, the groups watching gather that the resistors are about to destroy the statue in the town square. They light the fuse. Two young people, a girl and boy come in, without masks, from opposite sides. They are having a secret rendezvous. The resistance members are charmed by the young lovers and begin watching them with great interest. Suddenly one of them realizes that the bomb is about to go off and destroy not only the statue but also the lovers. A decision is made to quickly crawl over to the bomb and defuse it. The lovers leave. The resistance members quickly reset the bomb and are anxiously awaiting its explosion when the lovers return. This time the resistance members are a bit annoyed, and there is some debate about what to do. But then their sentiments win over and they again disarm the bomb.

This improvisation meets with Ariane Mnouchkine's approval. The high stakes of the situation, and the growing exasperation felt by the resistance members, as well as their choice to spare the lovers, was compelling. She congratulates the group on the timing of each action, the total commitment of the characters to their actions, and the different and specific qualities of the characters. She is especially impressed with how the actors remembered to share the mask, allowing the eyes of the characters to commune with the audience, complementing their expressive bodies. She praises how each has understood how to do the minimum to achieve the maximum, and thus has avoided filling the space with unnecessary gestures. She is particularly pleased with their ability to complete each action, to come to a full stop, and to take the time to finish before beginning the next action, to make form visible through rhythm – what she calls the basic work of all theater artists. Mnouchkine notes the group's ability to find both the individual leitmotif and rhythm of each character, as well as the collective rhythm of the small gang of resistors. Each effort at igniting the bomb was done differently, playing out the heightening tension of the situation. In addition, the lovers offered a beautifully drawn counterpoint of tenderness for each other, and obliviousness to anything around them.

Invasion and resistance

A group of Italian workshop participants volunteer the next improvisation. The Italian group takes up the masks of Pantalone and Arlecchino, mixing them with the dark, henna-colored Balinese mask of a dignified older man, sporting a wiry beard and a generous mouth. The latter mask enters onstage and looks up at the sky. The groups watching notice the sound of what seems to be a plane. Suddenly the plane enters coming in low and fast. The Arlecchino pilot is clearly a dare devil and his determined passengers are Mr and Mrs Pantalone, who hold on for dear life as the plane circles the field. The Pantalones land, map in hand, ready to invade this territory in search of buried treasure. The Balinese figure will be their guide. The Pantalones exude a single-minded need to control and dominate, but Arlecchino is bent on anarchy. The Pantalones' voices crackle with large expectations and big appetites. It is impossible to resist their drive and impatient self-interest. The Balinese figure looks at the map with great deliberation. He explains to them that the country has recently suffered a devastating war and that, according to this map, the treasure can only be reached by walking through a large mine field. The Pantalones are caught between their desire for self-preservation and their cupidity. Their overriding greed wins over and off they go through a maze of endless obstacles in hope of reaching their goal, with the Balinese figure calmly following behind with the map. Hearing the characters speaking Italian, one is struck by how powerfully the language suits the masks. Each explosive exhortation of the invaders is fraught with an almost operatic sensuality. The Pantolones are ruthless in their quest and in their need to outmaneuver even each other. Arlecchino's every movement suggests a mercurial intelligence as he resists their commands while still managing to obey. Throughout all this, the Balinese figure quietly but purposefully leads them on a wild goose chase.

Mnouchkine finds the commitment of the group to the physicality and emotional states of the characters both striking and instructive. The improvisation promotes a lesson in the quality of energy necessary to incarnate the rawness of humankind's desire for control, power, and wealth. She praises how Pantalone has been revealed through each rapport he manifests with the physical world: "It's all a question of his power." She is also impressed by the actors' economical use of text and their ability to create rests and stops, in order to feel the rhythm. She notes that action without hesitations, beginnings without endings, or confrontations without obstacles cannot be recognized as action.

Day 4: summing up and words of wisdom

The last day should include more improvisations and also the attempt to come to terms with what is often not yet understood. The participants will probably need to recall the following points:

- The purpose of the workshop is not to show off but to learn how difficult the art of working with masks is.
- The masks are indeed complete beings, so that one must also find the contradictions, as well as the basic lines. "You can't see the rays of the sun, if you can't see the dirt beneath you." Yet the masks are not odd and ugly creatures. There is beauty to be found in each.
- In this type of theater, monologue does not exist. One is always talking to someone, even if it is only the audience.
- One of the first steps in learning the craft of acting is the humble imitation of someone else whom one respects. To imitate, including imitating other beginning actors, is to recognize that all acting is teaching. But the imitation must start from the interior and not be a simple exterior copying.

- Above all, one must be careful not to break the magic of theater by touching one's mask or the mask of the other actors, to whom one must give space in order for the other actors to be fully present.

TO CONCLUDE

Ariane Mnouchkine would say that there are a few "secrets" to becoming an accomplished actor – in addition to hard work, humility, passion, and the willingness to voyage into the unknown. These are

- you must watch the great actors;
- observe life and you'll see it's not realistic;
- read the poets;
- imitate each other but not through caricature. Imitate the soul of the other;
- travel;
- work on your imagination;
- be simple;
- make space for your work.

A BASIC REHEARSAL VOCABULARY

Through the following vocabulary, we can grasp Mnouchkine's process as visual and imagistic rather than conceptual.

Concretizing: making concrete onstage a metaphor, the actors as sculptors of visual poetry.

Corporeal writing: writing onstage with the body, aiming for simplicity and readability.

Creation: in opposition to interpretation, which includes engaging the audience through discovery, working with – not for – the audience.

Godfathering/godmothering, twinning, or double teaming: when master actors/locomotives suggest approaches to characterization meant to be imitated by less experienced people, a privileged form of transmission through mimicry.

Interior music: a giving over to the truth of the mask/character, finding its profundity and uniqueness; Mnouchkine: "An actor must hear the music."

The obvious (*l'évidence*): the collective recognition of having arrived at the right gesture, character, or movement; when during improvisations the company sees as one.

Openness: the actor as empty space, letting the imagination work in order to free it, implicit in Mnouchkine's frequent exhortation, "Be concave!"

Physicality: Mnouchkine – "If it's not physical, it's not theatre."

Playing (to play): improvisations stressing lightness and pleasure; the theater itself must be an act of playfulness that in turn is a form of the sacred.

Presentness: staying completely in the moment of the stage action, including being present to all other actors' work, never abandoning theatricality.

Psychologizing: the worst approach to theater work, how to kill the process; hence Mnouchkine's admonishment: "The character isn't something you understand. It's something you work on until it's there."

Sacred space: the stage is another realm, a heightened reality, a privilege to be cherished, recognized, enjoyed.

The state (*l'état*) or internal landscape: the primary onstage emotional state, the in-the-moment state of being of the character; each state should contain something of the whole character, thus Mnouchkine's advice: "Look for the small to find the big!"; each state must be separated from the next.

The stop (or halt): crucial for marking each state onstage, for creating a visual rhythm.

Therapeutic friction: when an emotion bursts through unbidden in an improvisation and forms the basis for another improvisation.

A GLOSSARY OF TERMS
AND NAMES

Algerian War (1954–62)   The bloody conflict between Algerian nationalists and France that led to Algeria's independence, after some 150 years of colonial presence. What made this decolonization effort more complex and more difficult for the French, than many others, was the presence of over 1,000,000 European colonials in Algeria at the outset of the war and the fact that Algeria was officially an overseas department, thus part of France.

Althusser, Louis (1918–90)   A major Marxist intellectual of the post-Second World War period and supervising professor for the French national teaching degree, or *l'agrégation*, at the Ecole Normale Supérieure, France's most prestigious university for the humanities. His thinking about how ideology determines all human relationships and about how arts can politicize the masses anchored a great deal of the debate in France in the 1960s about the role of art in a changing society.

Avignon Theatre Festival (1947 to the present)   An annual, nearly month-long summer theater and dance festival showcasing the best in French, and of late, European theater and performance. Some 400 productions in the official and "off" festivals can be seen in venues ranging from the Honor Court of the Papal Palace to the ruins of the fourteenth-century fort in Villeneuve-lez-Avignon which once guarded "The City of the Popes." Founded and directed for twenty-four years by Jean Vilar, the Avignon Festival was a key player in the move to bring theater to all French citizens and thus to decentralize the arts.

Balinese masks (Topeng)   These wooden masks represent archetypal characters from the repertory of Balinese theater, much of which is based in the two significant epics of Hindu culture: the *Ramayana* and the *Mahabharata*. The origin of these masks probably dates back to the sixteenth century.

Barba, Eugenio (1927–)   Barba has long promoted intercultural theater from his theater laboratory, The Odin Theatre, in Scandinavia. A disciple of Grotowski, he regularly runs workshops introducing theatrical techniques from Asia, in particular, and he incorporates and blends many performance forms in his innovative and rigorous actor training.

Barrault, Jean-Louis (1910–94)   One of the principal directors of French theater in the late 1940s through the 1970s, Barrault was an accomplished mime performer and cinema actor. With his wife, the actor Madeleine Renaud, he introduced French audiences to the lyrical dramas of Claudel, while at the same time championing the playwrights of the so-called theater of the absurd – notably Beckett, Ionesco, and Vauthier.

Barthes, Roland (1915–80)   A multi-faceted and compelling thinker and critic. Having championed semiotic readings of texts, Barthes became a major promoter of political theater, and particularly, during the 1950s and 1960s, the theories of Bertolt Brecht through his participation in the influential theater review, *Théâtre Populaire* (1953–64).

Bharata natyam   A South-Indian dance form, originally danced in temples in honor of specific gods. The dance evolved into a form denoting and evoking sensuality and pleasure, characterized by intricate movement work with hands and feet and by energetic hip movements and glides. It often figures prominently in Bollywood films.

Bread and Puppet Theatre   From the 1960s, a US-based, international theater company that has long practiced collective creation and street theater forms of political activism, uniting puppetry with satirical denunciation.

Brecht, Bertolt (1898–1956)   With Antonin Artaud, the theoretician who has had the greatest influence on French theater production since the Second World War. His notions of, and techniques for, alienating or de-familiarizing audience members, so as to keep them from identifying with characters and experiencing emotional catharsis, were adopted by myriad companies in the 1960s in their quest for a viable political theater.

Brook, Peter (1925–)   Having established his theatrical laboratory (C.I.R.T.) in Paris in 1970, after a successful career as a stage and screen director in London, Brook proceeded to make of his international company, eventually housed at Les Bouffes du Nord, one of the most inspirational theatrical adventures of the twentieth century. He continues to be lauded for his discovery and promotion of new theatrical material and his inter-cultural experimentation, and for the philosophical urgency that fuels his theatrical mission.

Bunraku   A form of puppet theater characterized by meter-high marionettes each manipulated by three highly trained, black-costumed and hooded puppeteers (*koken*), clearly visible to the audience. A seated storyteller, capable of modulating his voice and changing register, sings and/or chants the various roles, accompanied by a string instrumentalist. All the artists contrive to disappear behind the marionettes, whose fingers, eyes, and mouths are articulated.

Chéreau, Patrice (1944–)   Having worked with Georgio Strehler in Milan in the late 1960s, Chéreau became a much-heralded theater director, especially during the 1970s and 1980s, completely revitalizing certain texts of Marivaux by a troubling psychoanalytical approach. He also introduced and interpreted to great acclaim the work of the now-deceased playwright Bernard-Marie Koltès. Of late, he is concentrating on productions of film and opera.

Commedia dell'arte   A highly physical theatrical form born in Italy and brought by traveling companies to France in the late sixteenth/early seventeenth centuries. *Commedia* depends on stock characters and improvised situations to capture broadly the central class conflicts that structure many Western cultures. Actors usually take as their own a particular role, including the mask and physical performance style that expresses it: Harlequin/Arlechino – the wily valet; Pantaloon/Pantalone – the greedy merchant; Pulchinello/Punch – the lower class, clever worker; El Dottore – the lubricous pedant, among others.

Decentralization   A significant government-subsidized movement organized to promote the arts outside of Paris that began in earnest in the late 1940s. It led in the 1960s, under Minister of Culture André Malraux, to the establishment of important cultural centers in the French provinces, and thus to a diversification of productions throughout France.

Dullin, Charles (1885–1949)   Arguably, the most important French inter-war theater director for his commitment to a pared-down staging, to physical stylization, and for his training of, and association with, numerous theater practitioners who transformed French theater after the war (Antonin Artaud, Jean-Louis Barrault, Roger Blin, Jean-Paul Sartre, Jean Vilar).

Enlightenment   The name given to the philosophical movement that dominated much of Western Europe, particularly France, England, and Germany, in the eighteenth century. The Enlightenment foregrounded rational thinking, logic, and scientific reasoning, while precluding faith, intuition, and reverie, as the best paths toward truth and social harmony, both in matters of metaphysics and government. It is believed by many that an overinvestment in, and a skewing of, enlightenment thinking helped propagate the West's sense of its intellectual and cultural superiority and thus abetted colonialism.

Foucault, Michel (1920–80)   A preeminent scholar of the workings of power and historical discourse, as well as a formidable activist and public intellectual, Foucault's thinking has had a crucial influence in understanding how social control and structures of domination become naturalized.

Genet, Jean (1910–86)   Perhaps the greatest of France's tradition of robber-poets, Genet was released from prison in the 1940s on the instigation of a committee of Parisian intellectuals. He went on to write in the late 1950s and 1960s some of France's richest plays, perverse rituals that put into question notions of character, plot, and theatrical propriety, notably *The Balcony* (1956), *The Blacks* (1958), and *The Screens* (1961), as well as to militate for the cause of The American Black Panther Party and for Palestinian rights.

Grotowski, Jerzy (1933–99)   Intimate friend of Peter Brook, author of *Towards a Poor Theatre* (1968), resonating with the theories of Artaud, founder of one of Poland's astonishing theatrical experiments, the Laboratory Theatre of Wroclaw, Grotowski's excruciatingly emotional and physical work was shown in France in the 1960s and 1970s and brought the French theater world ever closer to a theater based in extreme physical discipline. Grotowski-trained actors work on freeing themselves of all predictable reactions and movement patterns.

Hyper-real   An aesthetic categorization for that which appears, at first glance, to belong to the realist tradition, mimicking the everyday or photographic images, but which proves to be so heightened and so self-conscious that it moves into the realm of the symbolic.

Italianate space   The theatrical configuration still prevalent in Western theater, marked by a stage delimited by wings and a proscenium arch and by a seating plan that differentiates between closer seats (the orchestra), with better views, and less expensive seats farther from the stage and from the maximal viewing position. This stage–audience rapport reproduces the social hierarchy.

Jouvet, Louis (1887–1951)   One of four influential inter-war theater directors who called themselves The Cartel (Jouvet, Dullin, Gaston Baty, and Georges Pitoëff), Jouvet was determined to open up French theater to a new repertory and new techniques. He gave new life to French classical theater, particularly Molière, and partnered Jean Giraudoux through his exceptionally illuminating *mises-en-scène*. He was also an extraordinarily effective actor, giving shape to the most ominous aspects of the human psyche.

Kabuki   A highly coded Japanese theatrical form that dates roughly from the seventeenth century. Reinvigorated by borrowing plots from the marionette theater of Osaka and finding its core in dramas and comic riffs that treat the concerns of the rising middle class of Tokyo in the eighteenth century, kabuki boasts stylized acting and sumptuously costumed and heavily made-up performer/acrobats, the most admired often being female impersonators or *onnagato*.

Kantor, Tadeusz (1915–90)   A consummate artist, the Polish Kantor designed, constructed, directed, and wrote many of his surreal-istically charged theater pieces, most of which were marked by the horrors of living through the Second World War (fascism, violence, and concentration camps) and by an ambivalence toward the Catholic Church.

Kathakali   A majestic form of dance theater, based in ancient performed rites, such as the *kutiyattam*, and by the martial arts of southern India. Kathakali performers train from the time they are children in order to learn the hundreds of coded gestures, facial and eye movements, and choreographic figures that comprise the formal dimensions of their art. An onstage musical ensemble and singers who interpret the roles accompany performances, some of which can last throughout the night.

Lang, Jack (1939–)   Founder of the very influential Nancy Theatre Festival in the 1960s which brought to France avant-garde theater troupes from all over the world. Minister of Culture (1981–6; 1988–93) under Socialist President François Mitterand, Lang has devoted much of his career to promoting experimental and inter-nationalized art forms in France.

Lepage, Robert (1957–)   Quebecois actor and director, founder of one of Canada's most inventive theater collectives, Ex Machina, Lepage creates lengthy theatrical epics that grapple with deeply philosophical questions underpinning contemporary understandings of what makes for knowledge and nations.

Los desaparecidos   South American (particularly Argentine and Chilean) victims of state terrorism, kidnapping, and murder during the reign of military juntas in the 1970s and 1980s. In Argentina, notably, the mothers of "the disappeared" organized vigils to publicize their situation.

McBurney, Simon (1957–) Lecoq-trained theater actor and director, McBurney runs the London-based international collective, the Théâtre de Complicité, a company known for its physical and fluid stage presence where meaning is derived as much from stage sculpture and choreography as from text.

Mise-en-abîme The technique of embedding a formal construction within another formal construction *ad infinitum*.

Mise-en-scène The term for staging, that, in fact, indicates the act of conceptualization that goes into imagining not only movement patterns and performance style but also all of the design work, creating a total vision for the production. The term was invented in the latter half of the nineteenth century, along with the concept of the director or *metteur-en-scène*, a role still more powerful in theater work in France than in many other European countries.

Modernism An arts movement from the beginning of the twentieth century, especially taking form after the First World War, that elevated artistic expression to the highest endeavor to which humans could aspire, nearly a form of religious expression. The push was toward extreme creativity and inventiveness in order to refashion the world anew through experimentation with language and aesthetics. Representational conventions were violated in order to contest conventional notions of the world's coherency and of the unified position of the thinking and perceiving subject.

Noh A form of traditional Japanese theater, very much alive today and characterized by masked and heavily made-up actors in white face, by refined movements, stylized chanting, and a sense of ritual. Noh dates back to the medieval period in Japan and the goal of its lyrical pieces, composed by a series of master poets, is to transport the public to a hallucinatory realm, a space between the living and the nether world.

Orientalism The cultural practice of dominant Western countries of situating Eastern nations and regions, often colonized by the West and in any case less powerful in terms of economic and political control, as "other," different, and inferior, thus justifying to a certain extent their takeover by the West. Orientalism informs the representational practice of picturing the East as exotic and effeminate.

Planchon, Roger (1931–)   A key French theater director of the decentralization movement of the 1950s and 1960s, responsible at his National Theatre in Villeurbanne (Lyons) for inspiring a synthesis between the expressionist new theater of absurdist playwrights, such as Arthur Adamov, and the politicized practices of Bertolt Brecht. His *mises-en-scène* situate the classics of French theater in their historical context, conferring on them a political relevancy largely effaced in more traditional stagings. Planchon was central to a general rethinking of theatrical goals during the events of May 68.

Sartre, Jean-Paul (1905–80)   One of the main French playwrights of the 1950s and early 1960s, Sartre was also France's best known and most influential public intellectual after the Second World War. A prolific philosopher, as well as a writer of fiction, highly critical of the status quo, he championed freedom of expression and lifestyle, decolonization, and world democracy. His plays, while committed to voicing oppositional positions, were written within the conventions of French well-made dramas.

Strehler, Giorgio (1921–97)   Perhaps the greatest Italian director of the twentieth century, known for the brilliance of his stage pictures and the beauty of his vast theatrical canvasses, as well as for his complete control of the staging process, Strehler animated for many years, from 1947 until his death, with Paolo Grassi, one of Italy's foremost theaters, the Piccolo Theatre of Milan. There, he brought back to life in his partnership with Amleto Sartori *commedia dell'arte* performance, which had been neglected for over a century. He also founded and directed in the 1980s France's Théâtre de l'Europe, a theatrical forum for showcasing the most interesting theatrical work on the continent. His influence on European staging is immense.

Théâtre des Nations   From 1954 to 1968, this state-subsidized producing venture presented at the Châtelet Theatre in Paris an extra-ordinary variety of international work, including the Peking Opera, the Moscow Arts Theatre, The Abbey Theatre, Balinese dance, kabuki, Noh, and bunraku, and productions by directors Visconti, Brook, and Brecht. Its influence on French theater people was enormous, helping to renew acting styles, develop approaches to total theater, and foster the importance of a stage language based on gestures.

Théâtre National Populaire   The idea of a national popular theater, or a state-subsidized theater for the people, had been importantly in play in France since an early attempt at such an institution in the 1920s. The most successful iteration evolved under Jean Vilar, named to head the T.N.P. in Paris in 1951. His aim was to bring well-known classical pieces, as well as new texts, through devices such as lowering ticket prices and working with unions, to a broad range of French spectators, but especially to those people deprived of the opportunity of going to the theater. Vilar left the T.N.P. in 1963; and in 1972 the T.N.P. was relocated to Villeurbanne, under Roger Planchon.

Western self   This notion, more and more contested, nevertheless frames certain widely accepted tenets of what constitutes Western identity and civilization, including Judeo-Christian values, representative government and democracy, scientific progress, and free market enterprise.

Zeami (*c.*1363–1443)   One of the finest playwrights of Noh theater (some fifty plays), hailed for moving it ever more toward a form of dream work. His treatises on acting, stressing extreme technical, intellectual, and physical concentration, are still studied.

BIBLIOGRAPHY

THEATER TEXTS

Cixous, Hélène (1985) *L'Histoire terrible mais inachevée de Norodom Sihanouk, roi du Cambodge*, Paris: Théâtre du Soleil.

—— (1987) *L'Indiade ou l'Inde de leurs rêves et quelques écrits sur le théâtre*, Paris: Théâtre du Soleil.

—— (1994a) *The Terrible but Unfinished Story of Norodom Sihanouk, King of Cambodia* (trans. Juliet Flower MacCannell, Judith Pike, and Lollie Groth), Lincoln and London: University of Nebraska Press.

—— (1994b) *La Ville Parjure ou le réveil des Erinyes*, Paris: Théâtre du Soleil.

—— (1999) *Tambours sur la digue: Sous forme de pièce ancienne pour marionnettes, jouée par des acteurs*, Paris: Théâtre du Soleil.

—— (2004a) "Drums on the Dam: In the Form of an Ancient Puppet Play Performed by Actors" (trans. Brian J. Mallet and Judith G. Miller) in Prenowitz, Eric (ed.) *Selected Plays of Hélène Cixous*, London: Routledge, 191–221.

—— (2004b) "The Perjured City or the Awakening of the Furies" (trans. Bernadette Fort) in Prenowitz, Eric (ed.) *Selected Plays of Hélène Cixous*, London: Routledge, 89–190.

Mnouchkine, Ariane (1979) *Méphisto, le roman d'une carrière*, Paris: Solin/Théâtre du Soleil.

—— (1990) "Méphisto" (trans. Timberlake Wertenbaker) in *Theatre and Politics: An International Anthology*, New York: Ubu Repertory Theatre Publications, 361–469.

Shakespeare, William (1984) *Richard II* (trans. Ariane Mnouchkine), Paris: Théâtre du Soleil.

Théâtre du Soleil (1971a) *1789: La révolution doit s'arrêter à la perfection du bonheur*, Paris: Stock.

—— (1971b) "1789" (trans. Alexander Trocchi) *Gambit* 5(20): 5–52.

—— (1972) *1793: La cite révolutionnaire est de ce monde*, Paris: Stock.

—— (1975) *L'Age d'Or: Première ébauche*, Paris: Stock.

—— (1989) *1789 et 1793*, Paris: Théâtre du Soleil.

—— (1989) *1789: Profile d'une oeuvre*, Schwartz, Helmut and Wandel, Helga (eds), Frankfurt: Diesterweg.

BOOKS, JOURNALS, AND INTERVIEWS

Alter, Jean (1998) "Decoding Mnouchkine's Shakespeares" in Issacharoff, Michael and Jones, Robin (eds) *Performing Texts*, Philadelphia, PA: University of Pennsylvania Press, 75–85.

Artaud, Antonin (1958) *The Theater and Its Double*, trans. Mary C. Richard, New York: Grove Press.

Atack, Margaret (1999) *May 68 in French Fiction and Film: Rethinking Society, Rethinking Representation*, Oxford: Oxford University Press.

Bablet, Denis and Marie-Louise (1979) *Le Théâtre du Soleil (Diapolivre)*, Paris: C.N.R.S.

Banu, Georges (2000) "Nous, les marionnettes . . . le bunraku fantasmé du Théâtre du Soleil," *Alternatives Théâtrales* 65(66): 68–70.

Berger, Anne, Cornell, Sarah, Salesne, Pierre, Sandré, Marguerite, and Setti, Nadia (eds) (1984) "En plein soleil," *Fruits* 2(3): whole issue.

Bradby, David (1991) *Modern French Drama 1940–1990*, Cambridge: Cambridge University Press.

Bradby, David and Delgado, Maria (eds) (2002) *The Paris Jigsaw*, Manchester: Manchester University Press.

Bradby, David and Williams, David (1988) *Directors' Theatre*, New York: St Martin's Press.

Carré, Françoise (1985) "Les Rescapés du Soleil," *Autrement* 70: 146–51.

Cixous, Hélène (1983) *Le Livre de Promethea*, Paris: Gallimard.

Copfermann, Emile (1971) "Entretiens avec Ariane Mnouchkine et le Soleil: Différent – Le Théâtre du Soleil," *Travail Théâtral* Lausanne (La Cité): 3–33.

Delgado, Maria and Heritage, Paul (eds) (1996) *In Contact with the Gods: Directors Talk Theatre*, Manchester, Manchester University Press.

Dort, Bernard (1973) "l'Histoire jouée," *Avant-Scène Théâtre* 526(7): 9–16.

Double Page 21 (1982) *Le Théâtre du Soleil: Shakespeare*: photos de Martine Franck, Paris: Editions SNEP.

Double Page 32 (1984) *Le Théâtre du Soleil: Shakespeare 2*: photos de Martine Franck, Paris: Editions SNEP.

Double Page 49 (1987) *Le Théâtre du Soleil: L'Indiade:* photos de Martine Franck, Paris: Editions SNEP.

Dusigne, Jean-François (2003) *Le Théâtre du Soleil: Des Traditions orientales à la modernité occidentale*, Paris: Centre National de Documentation Pédagogique.

Féral, Josette (1998) *Trajectoires du Soleil: Autour d'Ariane Mnouchkine*, Paris: Editions Théâtrales.

—— (2001) *Dresser un monument à l'éphémère: Rencontres avec Ariane Mnouchkine*, Paris: Editions Théâtrales.

Fischer-Lichte, Erika, Riley, Josephine, and Gissenwehrer, Michael (eds) (1970) *The Dramatic Touch of Difference: Theatre, Own and Foreign*, Tubingen: Gunter Narr Verlag Tubingen.

Hewlett, Nicholas (ed.) (2003) *The Cambridge Companion to Modern French Culture*, Cambridge: Cambridge University Press.

Innes, Christopher (1993) *Avant-Garde Theatre 1892–1992*, Paris: Routledge.

Issacharoff, Michael and Jones, Robin (eds) (1998) *Performing Texts*, Philadelphia, PA: University of Pennsylvalnia Press.

Kiernander, Adrian (1992) "Reading (,) Theatre (,) Techniques: Responding to the Influence of Asian Theatre in the Work of Ariane Mnouchkine," *Modern Drama* 35: 322–33.

—— (1993) *Ariane Mnouchkine and the Théâtre du Soleil*, Cambridge: Cambridge University Press.

Labrouche, Laurence (1999) *Ariane Mnouchkine: Un parcours théâtral (Le terrassier, l'enfant et le voyageur)*, Paris: l'Harmattan.

Lecoq, Jacques (ed.) (1987) *Le Théâtre du geste: Mimes et acteurs*, Paris: Bordas.

Les Voies de la création théâtrale V (1977) *1793, l'Age d'Or*, Paris: CNRS Editions.

Maranca, Bonnie and Dasgupta, Gautem (eds) (1991) *Interculturalism and Performance: Writings from PAJ*, New York: PAJ Publications.

Miller, Judith G. (1977) *Theatre and Revolution in France Since 1968*, Lexington: French Forum Monographs.

Mnouchkine, Ariane and Penchenat, Jean-Claude (1971) "L'Aventure du Théâtre du Soleil," *Preuves* 7: 119–27.

Nelson, Victoria (2001) *The Secret Life of Puppets*, London: Harvard.

Neuschafer, Anne (2002) *De l'Improvisation au rite: L' épopée de notre temps: Le Théâtre du Soleil au Carrefour des genres*, Frankfurt sur Main: Peter Lang.

Pascaud, Fabienne (2005) *Ariane Mnouchkine: Entretiens avec Fabienne Pascaud*, Paris: Plon.

Pavis, Patrice (1992) *Theatre at the Crossroads of Culture* (trans. Loren Kruger), London: Routledge.

—— (ed.) (1996) *The Intercultural Performance Reader*, London: Routledge.

Perret, Jean (1987) "Entretien avec Ariane Mnouchkine" in Lecoq, Jacques (ed.) *Le Théâtre du geste: Mimes et acteurs*, Paris: Bordas, 127–30.

Picard, Anne-Marie (1989) "*l'Indiade*, Ariane's and Hélène's Conjugate Dream," *Modern Drama* 32: 24–38.

Picon-Vallin, Béatrice (2000) "Le Soleil, de *Soudain des nuits d'éveil* à *Tambours sur la digue*: Les longs cheminements de la troupe du Soleil," *Théâtre Public* 152: 4–13.

Prenowitz, Eric (ed.) (2004) *Selected Plays of Hélène Cixous*, London: Routledge.

Quillet, Françoise (1999) *L'Orient au théâtre du soleil*, Paris: l'Harmattan.

Richardson, Helen (1990) "The Théâtre du Soleil and the Quest for Popular Theatre in the Twentieth Century," (PhD dissertation), The University of California, Berkeley.

Salter, Denis (1993) "Hand, Eye, Mind, Soul: Théâtre du Soleil's *Les Atrides*," *Theatre Magazine* 24(1): 59–74.

Samary, Jean-Jacques and Thibaudet, Jean-Pierre (1984) "l'Ombre d'Ariane dans le soleil: Entretien avec Philippe Hottier et Georges Bigot," *Libération* 12(July): 28–9.

Scheie, Timothy (1994) "Body Trouble: Corporeal Presence and Performative Identity in Cixous's and Mnouchkine's *Indiade*," *Theatre Journal* 46(1): 31–44.

Sellers, Susan (ed.) (1994) *The Hélène Cixous Reader*, London: Routledge.

Shevtsova, Maria (1995) "*La Ville Parjure*: Entretien avec Ariane Mnouchkine," *Alternatives Théâtrales* 48: 69–73.

Tatlow, Anthony (2001) *Shakespeare, Brecht, and the Intercultural Sign*, Durham: Duke University Press.

Théâtre du Soleil (1990) *Les Atrides* 1: photos de Michèle Laurent.

—— (1992) *Les Atrides* 2: photos de Michèle Laurent.

Van Rossum-Guyon, Françoise and Diaz-Diocaretz, Myriam (eds) (1991) *Hélène Cixous: Chemin d'une écriture*, Paris: Presses Universitaires de Vincennes.

Williams, David (ed.) (1999) *Collaborative Theatre: The Théâtre du Soleil Sourcebook*, London: Routledge.

VIDEOS AND FILMOGRAPHY

Darmon, Eric and Vilpoux, Catherine with Mnouchkine, Ariane (1997) *Au Soleil même la nuit*, Paris: Agat Films/La Sept ARTE/ Théâtre du Soleil.

Mnouchkine, Ariane (1974) *1789*, Paris: les Films Ariane.

—— (1976–7) *Molière ou la vie d'un honnête homme*, Paris: Les Films du Soleil de la Nuit/Claude Lelouche; 2004 DVD, Paris: Bel Air Classiques/SCEREN-CNDP.

—— /Théâtre du Soleil (1980) *La Nuit miraculeuse* (dialogues by Hélène Cixous), Paris: France Telecom/La Mission du Bicentenaire/*et al.*

—— (2002) *Tambours sur la digue: Sous forme de pièce ancienne pour marionettes jouée par des acteurs*, Paris: Le Théâtre du Soleil/ARTE France/Bel Air Media.

—— (2006) *Le Dernier Caravansérail (Odyssées)*, Paris: Bel Air Classiques/SCEREN-CNDP.

Vilpoux, Catherine (1999) *Film d'après La Ville Parjure ou le réveil des Erinyes*, Paris: Vidéo de Poche/Le Théâtre du Soleil.

MUSIC

Lemêtre, Jean-Jacques (1985) *L'Histoire terrible mais inachevée de Norodom Sihanouk, roi du Cambodge: musique du spectacle*, Théâtre du Soleil (tape recorded at La Cartoucherie).

—— (1987) *L'Indiade ou l'Inde de leurs rêves: musique du spectacle*, Théâtre du Soleil (tape recorded at La Cartoucherie).

—— (1991) *Les Danses d'Iphigénie à Aulis d'Euripide et Agamemnon d'Eschyle, Les Atrides 1*, Théâtre du Soleil.

—— (1992a) *Musique du spectacle Agamemnon d'Eschyle*, Théâtre du Soleil.

—— (1992b) *Musique du spectacle les Choéphores d'Eschyle*, Théâtre du Soleil.

—— (1992c) *Musique du spectacle Iphigénie à Aulis d'Euripide*, Théâtre du Soleil.

—— (1993) *Musique du spectacle les Euménides d'Eschyle*, Théâtre du Soleil.

—— (1999) *Et Soudain des Nuits d'éveil: musique du spectacle*, Théâtre du Soleil (CD recorded by Yann Lemêtre at the Cartoucherie).

—— (2000) *Tambours sur la digue: sous forme de pièce ancienne pour marionnettes jouée par des acteurs: musique du spectacle*, Théâtre du Soleil (CD recorded by Yann Lemêtre at the Cartoucherie).

INDEX

Note: Page numbers in **bold** refer to figures

Related titles from Routledge

Theatre Histories:
An Introduction

Edited by Philip B. Zarrilli, Bruce McConahie,
Gary Jay Williams and Carol Fisher Sorgenfrei

'This book will significantly change theatre education'
Janelle Reinelt, *University of California, Irvine*

Theatre Histories: An Introduction is a radically new way of looking at both
the way history is written and the way we understand performance.

The authors provide beginning students and teachers with a clear, exciting
journey through centuries of Eurpoean, North the South American,
African and Asian forms of theatre and performance.

Challenging the standard format of one-volume theatre history texts, they
help the reader think critically about this vibrant field through fascinating
yet plain-speaking essays and case studies.

Among the topics covered are:

- representation and human expression
- interpretation and critical approaches
- historical method and sources
- communication technologies
- colonization
- oral and literate cultures
- popular, sacred and elite forms of performance.

Keeping performance and culture very much centre stage, *Theatre Histories:
An Introduction* is compatible with standard play anthologies, full of
insightful pedagogical apparatus, and comes accompanied by web site
resources.

ISBN HB: 978–0–415–22727–8
ISBN PB: 978–0–415–22728–5

**Available at all good bookshops
For ordering and futher information please visit:
www.routledge.com**